Dea[r] ♡
Thank you for coming.
Thank you for sharing.
Thank you for listening.
Thank you for loving –
As always –
My love
Rita

... *I Love You, Mom*

(the thoughts I wanted to share and didn't because you were either too young to understand or too old to listen)

Rita Grill Pope

Fairway Press, Lima, Ohio

... I LOVE YOU, MOM

FIRST EDITION

ISBN 0-7880-1620-2

PRINTED IN U.S.A.

I dedicate this book to —

— my mother, for her unconditional love and support

— my children, Paula, Rita and Stephen, for their encouragement, inspiration and love

— my dear friend, Bill, who always believed in me

— all mothers and children of any age who are looking for understanding and love

Dear Love,

The house is strangely quiet. There are no phones madly ringing; no minute to minute schedules for me to juggle; no young feet taking the stairs two at a time; or, frantic calls for my help in averting a last minute disaster.

In the last several years, I have seen each of you move on to lives of your own. What greater achievement can a mother reach than to see her life's work bear fruit — to see you strong, independent and capable of beginning your adult lives with anticipation, determination and excitement!

The realization has finally sunk in, as I closed the door behind the latest moving van, that my job as your mother is just about over. You, my love, are on your own, and after nearly a quarter of a century, I am alone. I have had hung over my desk, for many years, this saying: THERE ARE ONLY TWO LASTING BEQUESTS WE CAN HOPE TO GIVE OUR CHILDREN. ONE OF THESE IS ROOTS, THE OTHER, WINGS.* All these years, as I have carefully planted and tended little roots, I have jokingly talked with you about my excitement in seeing "my little birds" fly one day. This was my way of preparing you to take these final steps, and it was also my way of reminding myself that the day would come and you would be gone. The day is here now. I want you to know that it is a breathtaking sight for me to see you soar high into the skies of your lives, sometimes on shaky wings, then, after a few moments of faltering, soar once again, with renewed confidence. You have made it, and, in my own way, I have completed the tasks that I set out to do.

I know that it is time for me to turn my back on the sight of you flying off into the distance, and I know that it is time for me to start down new roads that lay ahead of me. Paradoxically, it is a time that I have looked forward to and dreaded at the same time. I find myself unable to take the first step, however, until I complete one final task as your mother.

During the years of your life, I have had so many thoughts that I wanted to tell you about, but the timing just was never right.

When you were small, the thoughts were too grown-up for you to understand; when you were grown-up, the thoughts were too small for you to bother listening to.

Over the years, I buried these thoughts in my mind and heart, and, periodically, I would write them down on scraps of paper to be compiled at a later date into what has become referred to as "Mom's Book." Now is the time, before I move down totally new roads, that I want to reflect and write down for you the things that I was thinking over the years.

There are no earth-shattering thoughts in these pages. They are the simple thoughts that arose as the by-product of the simple experiences of my life as your mother. They are my final gift to each of you. They will tell you, not only what I was thinking and who I was as a person during the mothering years, but, they will also tell you much about a mother's perspective on life.

I offer to you, my love, these simple thoughts, reflections, observations and stories which have marked my simple life and yours.

I love you, Mom

*Anonymous Quote

Dear Love,

As children we would go down to the pond in the middle of the nearby park and skip stones across the surface of the water. After many attempts at skipping stones, I became very proficient at this activity. I always found it fascinating to watch the ripples which ensued, when I skipped the stones just right across the waters of the pond.

I had a teacher in college who used to say, "Every human contact is an infinite responsibility." This statement describes the ripple effect of skipping stones in our daily lives perfectly.

Every human contact, no matter how big or small, just like skipping a stone across the water, can create a ripple effect on the life of another human being. That kind word said to a rather surly check-out clerk, that smile to an elderly person encountered on the street, that spontaneous "I love you" to an overwrought parent, can create ripples which lift spirits and make lives worthwhile.

We, who know how to skip stones, need to practice the art with everyone we encounter. Those, that do not know how to skip stones, need to go down to the nearest pond and learn. It is our infinite responsibility and an art that every human being should practice.

I love you, Mom

Dear Love,

Curled up on the sofa last night, I watched a superior actress perform a wonderful role in a rather mediocre play. "Why," I thought, "would such a fine actress take part in a production that was obviously not of a high caliber?"

Actors and actresses have the right to peruse a script before they decide to play a particular role. Many times in perusing a "not-so-good script", an actor or actress will find one redeeming feature in an otherwise inferior play, which will convince them to invest time and energy in playing a role in a play which might only run for one night.

As human beings, we have no right of perusal when it comes to the scripts of our lives. We invest our time and energy in various roles, never knowing ahead of time if, in theatrical terms, our play will run for only one night, or, will, in a sense, be a Broadway hit.

I want you, my children, to know that if I had perused the script of my life ahead of time, I might never have taken the part I have played for so many years **except** for one redeeming feature — that redeeming feature was the honor and privilege of playing the role of your mother. It has been the most important role of my life.

I love you, Mom

Dear Love,

Grandma's thirteen year old dog, Patches, has come to live with us because she could no longer take care of him. He is laying by my feet at this moment, and hasn't moved more than two feet away from me since I brought him home yesterday.

Patches was adopted by Grandma when he was about three years old. He had been an orphan of the storm. Someone had left this gentle creature to die, tied to a tree, deep in the Forest Preserve, where no one could find him.

As I look into his tired, sad, brown eyes — just about covered over with cataracts — I know instinctively why I took him in. I did not want him to be left homeless in his old age and to die alone. He really doesn't require much care — just a bowl of water, some food, a warm place to lay down, and a hand to pet his head once in awhile. In return, he is giving me companionship and undying loyalty.

Now that I think of it, what he is giving me in his final days in return for his care, is worth far more than anything I could give to him.

I love you, Mom

Dear Love,

As I drove to your aunt's home in the country this morning, I grumpily noted the foreboding weather. It was gray and raw outside with that dampness that penetrates your bones and sends shivers up and down your spine — no matter how many layers of clothing you have on.

The sky was crowded with huge, ominous-looking, dark-gray clouds. "Hmmm", I thought to myself, "I hope that I return home before those clouds dump their load of winter snow on the highway." I was not in the mood for snow today; all the fuss and bother of slippery, treacherous roads; foggy car windows inside; and, clattering windshield wipers that never push the snow away fast enough.

As I was thrashing around mentally, a jagged slit opened up in the foreboding clouds and the whole landscape changed. In this opening, a giant, almost iridescent orb appeared, thinly veiled with a transparent layer of cloudy substance. Generating from the orb were countless, silvery streaks of light, reaching toward the earth in an all-encompassing, cone-shaped arrangement as if fingers of mystical light were pointing the way.

The vision was breathtaking, and as I kept driving in awe-struck amazement, a sense of calm and peace settled over me. Even though my faith is shaky at times, I knew instinctively that I had seen the hand of God in that opening in the clouds.

I love you, Mom

Dear Love,

Without a doubt — I am a cryer ! Not a town crier as in Paul Revere — but an honest-to-goodness, right from the pit of the stomach, "cryer". Growing up, I just about drove my unemotional father crazy whenever I would cry. He would exclaim with frustration at the never-ending waterworks,"Rita, stop crying! Your kidneys must be connected to your tear ducts!" Even my brothers and sisters gave me a hard time about my crying. They endlessly told me that when I grew up, I would be a professional mourner and hire out for weddings and funerals — any occasion that needed a few tears.

My crying used to embarrass me but it doesn't anymore. My ability to cry, I've come to feel, is a wonderful trait. It has helped me to bury hurts and resentments; it has helped me forgive people that I otherwise might not forgive; and, it has helped me share my feelings with others. I believe that crying is a catharsis for the soul — cleansing, healing and refreshing, like clean, rain water running down a muddy street. I feel that if we had a few more people in the world who could cry, we wouldn't have so many angry, hostile people running around taking their aggressions out on innocent people who happen to cross their paths. The world, then, might be a happier, although definitely soggier, place for all of us.

I love you, Mom

Dear Love,

This was the house of my dreams — a beautiful, hundred year old Victorian house with about a hundred years of problems and decorating that came with it. I took the job of rehabbing it myself because of lack of funds.

One of the rehabbing jobs was to repaint the beautiful staircase. It took me weeks, a little bit at a time, to paint my way from the bottom balustrade to the top balustrade. In my haste, when I finally reached the top landing, I moved the gallon of paint just a little, too close to the edge of the top stair and — you guessed it — I bumped it and watched in horror as it tumbled down the length of the staircase. It spread white paint over every stair, dumping the bottom of the gallon of paint on the Oriental rug in the hall below. The clean-up job was incredible and took hours of backbreaking labor.

This was a mess to end all messes. However, I would never have considered leaving the mess for anyone else to clean-up. I would never have given up my beautiful house just because of this mess. I would never have pretended that it never existed and found something else to do.

A self-made mess is a mess that has to be cleaned-up by the person who made it in the first place. Leaving a mess for someone else to clean-up is unconscionable. Giving up everything worked for, just because of one mess, leaves you with nothing and solves nothing. Walking away from a mess and pretending it isn't there, does not make it go away, but leaves it there to harden and become a more difficult mess to clean-up.

The lesson I learned from dealing with this horrendous mess is this: When you make a mess, roll up your sleeves immediately; assess how you are going to clean it up; and, start cleaning it up until the task is completed.

I love you, Mom

Dear Love,

The night was a typical cold, windy, January night. The streets were slick with the endless drizzle of rain which had not stopped for two days. If it had been cold enough for snow, the streets would have been buried in mountains of it.

As the teenage boys drove up the highway ramp, a scraggly figure could be made out in the distance, dressed only in torn jeans and a T-shirt on this miserable night, and carrying a handmade sign which read, "I am homeless. Can you help me?" No one paid any attention to this unwanted person as car after car went by, until your brother drove up the ramp with his friends. Without a moments hesitation, he gave the homeless figure, the ten dollars he had in his pocket, which was all he had for his night out. His friends told him that he was stupid because "he" would probably just use it to buy booze. Your brother's reply, "Well, I guess we'll never know whether he spends it on booze or gets something to eat with it, will we?" It was worth the risk to him.

He came in early that night and went to bed. You can't do much with no money in your pocket. As I sat in the kitchen by myself after he told me the story and went to bed, my eyes caught a saying I have had hung on the wall since you were all babies. It reads:

I shall pass through this world but once. If, therefore, there be any kindness I can show or good thing I can do, let me do it now; let me not defer or neglect it...for I shall not pass this way again.*

I have often wondered if anyone ever read any of the quotes I have hung on the walls in the house. I know now that your brother has read this one.

I love you, Mom

*Based on an Anonymous quote

Dear Love,

I was cleaning under the radiator the other day and came up with a very dirty, forlorn, little person — a "weeble" — left behind by some previous tenant of the house. What is a weeble? Twenty years ago, when you were little, weebles were one of the most popular toys of your generation. They were little, egg-shaped people, similar to a stand-up punching bag, and advertised as, "Weebles, wobble, but they don't fall down."

Years ago, I used to wonder what was in a weeble that made weebles wobble and not fall down. I never did find out what was in a weeble body that gave it this wonderfully, resilient quality. I have discovered, however, a truth of life in my little wobbly, weeble person.

We all have the potential to be weeble people in our lives if we look hard within ourselves. I may not know what makes weebles so remarkably resilient in posture, but, I do know, that if our lives are grounded in truth, honesty, loyalty, love, understanding and forgiveness, we can all be weeble people — able to take the hurts and blows in life, and maybe wobble a bit, but not fall down for very long.

I have decided to give this weeble a bath and give it a new home as a reminder of this truism. Little does he know the value he represents.

I love you, Mom

Dear Love,

Periodically, I go on the "getting rid-of, throwing out" rampage. After years of living with "things", that at one time I thought I couldn't live without, I, all of a sudden, want to get the biggest garbage bag that I can find, and throw everything into it until I am stripped clean of "things."

I am always amazed after one of these rampages, at how I categorize things "to keep or to throw out." It seems that the things that I own that have monetary value, I would give to the lowest bidder in a garage sale; and, the things that I own that have no monetary value, I wouldn't part with for anything. It's ironic that this is a total one hundred and eighty degree turn-around from thirty plus years ago.

In my collection of things "to keep" are three special favorites: a Christmas tree, decorated with clumsily, hand-cut paper ornaments, enclosed precariously in a little glass dome; three, little, chubby Japanese figures with bright red, painted lips; and, an original poetry framed in plastic.

Ivory, jade, crystal, china, silver, antiques and fine artwork are all things I could throw out today, with not a thought as to their monetary value. At this stage in my life, I want only those precious, priceless treasures around me that were your gifts to me over the years. These are the only real treasures that I own because they are tied up with my memories of you. I will carry these treasures with me forever.

I love you, Mom

Dear Love,

A colossal, inflated Santa Claus loomed over my car this morning as I was on my way to the grocery store. On his jolly, old stomach, a sign was posted — "Christmas in July Sale." My first reaction was "Christmas in July!!! The last thing I want to think of is Christmas in July!!!" However, as I drove along, I thought, "Why not? We should be selling Christmas in July, October, January, April — every month — all year long!" I forgot all about going to the grocery store, turned the car around, and headed for home to begin my campaign in the neighborhood to sell Christmas all year long.

When I arrived home, I headed to the attic; dug around in the boxes marked "Xmas Decorations"; and, pulled out four strings of tangled outdoor lights. Out to the backyard bush I went to hang them, and bring a message of Christmas to everyone in the neighborhood in this month of July.

Tonight, I am a Christmas salesman, as I stand in awe in front of my twinkling bush. I hope in time, it will bring the message to all who see it that the Christmas gifts of love, forgiveness and understanding, lived out all year, are those things which bring us from un-wise men to wise men in our journey through life and insure peace and goodwill to all — all year round. Merry Christmas! Even if it is July!

I love you, Mom

Dear Love,

Getting children to bed is a hassle for any parent. It was no different in our home. As the magic hour of bedtime approached, there were always a million excuses to try and stay up later than the designated hour. Nonetheless, I always eventually mananged to get you all into bed.

After making sure that your favorite blanket or stuffed animal was in your arms, tucking in loose blankets, we would always say your bedtime prayers as part of this night time ritual. I knew at that time that you had no idea of the meaning of the words that you were carefully repeating after me. My hope, however, was that you would remember these words we said nightly and live them out in your life. Our night time prayer went like this:

Lord, Make me an instrument of your peace.
Where there is hatred, let me sow love; where there is injury, pardon; where there is doubt, faith; where there is despair, hope; where there is darkness, light; where there is sadness, joy.

O Divine Master, grant that I may not so much seek to be consoled as to console; to be understood, as to understand; to be loved as to love; for it is in giving that we receive; in pardoning that we are pardoned; in dying that we are born to eternal life. Amen.*

As I watch you move into life, I know that these words have stayed with you.

I love you, Mom

*St. Francis of Asissi

Dear Love,

A very special cup and saucer is sitting in a prominent place on the counter in my kitchen. It is iridescent blue and silver in color, with a high-footed bottom and a double-looped handle, all edged in gold. The saucer mirrors the cup in color and style. It is one-of-a-kind, at least I think so.

This dainty cup is my favorite cup because you bought it for me one Christmas. I do not live the daintiest or most regal life but every morning I feel like a queen when I pour my coffee into it. As I enjoy, my first few sips out of my very special cup, my thoughts always go to you, no matter where you are. In this way, I am reminded that I am as special to you as you are to me.

I love you, Mom

Dear Love,

The weather has been unusually warm for this time of year. The yard has new activity in it — more appropriate for spring, than for winter. For several days now, I have been watching the progress of a large, black spider building a web in the corner of the garage. Two days ago, the web was only as big as the palm of my hand, but the warm, winter sun must have encouraged the spider to expand the territory of the web in hopes of catching a nice, juicy fly for dinner. Last evening, the spider had achieved his goal because tangled up in the web was just that — a nice, juicy fly !

I went out this afternoon to see what was going on by the garage door with my insect friends. To my surprise, I found that the weight of the spider and his prey had pulled the entire web down from its place near the garage roof. Both, the fly and the spider, were now trapped by the fallen web.

As I walked away, I thought to myself, "This is why as human beings we should never build webs of lies in our lives. Webs of lies only bring momentary reward and pleasure. Eventually, a web of lies comes down of its own weight and traps everyone in a tangled mess — weaver and victim alike. Sadly, no one escapes. Let my insects friends be a warning to all of us.

I love you, Mom

Dear Love,

I love to walk alone at night, despite the protests I hear about this nocturnal idiosyncrasy of mine. I suppose it isn't safe. However, I feel that what could happen under the starlit sky, around some darkened corner or behind some towering tree, could just as well happen under the glaring sunlight of a cloudless, blue sky in a neighborhood shopping center.

I walk at night because this is a time when there is no hustle and bustle of street activity; when I can write fairy tales in my mind and always be the princess; when I try to figure out the enigmas in life that have no answers; when I can feel joyous about some nonsensical achievement; or grieve over some slight disappointment. Night is my contemplative time. The day's activities are completed. It is time to synthesize the moments that have passed in twenty-four hours. It is time to appreciate those moments that will be no more, but, are now, single threads in the weaving of my life.

Walking at night, I have learned to acknowledge that endless night is always waiting for all of us, not like some black-hooded figure with a sickle in hand, but like a gentle person waiting to take that final walk with us.

No, I am not afraid to walk alone at night, and so, once again, I put on my walking shoes to begin my evening ritual — my nightly sojourn toward eternity.

I love you, Mom

Dear Love,

Princess Alexandra was not a sought after member of our household. In fact, until she came to live with us, I had a total aversion to cats. To my thinking, they were sneaky, little creatures that lurched around corners, and really wanted nothing to do with human beings. I was a confirmed "dog only" person — or — so I thought.

Princess Alexandra is an orange, tabby cat with eyes the same color as her fur. She landed on my doorstep because she could not be kept in a college dorm. As a result of her presence in our household, I have done a one hundred and eighty degree turn around on my opinion of cats.

Ally has now become my shadow and where I go in the house, she goes with me. There isn't much I can do without finding Ally right in the middle of it. I always know when there is a lump in the bed that somehow she has found her way under the clean sheets. No matter where she is in the house, she always hears the pouring of coffee — knowing that she will receive a few drops from the milk pitcher. Then, there are those daily serenades on the piano keys as she walks across them, and the wild kitty routine when she runs through the house, using everything as a springboard.

Needless to say, Ally is all over the place. There are telltale bits of evidence that tell you "Ally was here" — little paw prints on dusty tables, and clothes studded with orange hairs . However, I always smile to myself when I find these signs, and I think, "Unconditional love roams in my house." Ally doesn't care how I look or what I have on. She loves me just because "I am."

I love you, Mom

Dear Love,

Even at this age, when you are hurt, I feel the "Mother Hen" instinct rise up in me. I want to charge into the barnyard, flap my wings and chase away whoever or whatever is hurting you. However, I am no longer there to wrap you safely in my arms. I can no longer dry the tears and kiss the hurts to make them go away. I no longer have the magical power to give you reasons as to why bad things happen; why there is pain in your world; and, why there are questions that loom in your mind for which there are no answers.

I only know that the dark threads of your life are being interwoven with the bright threads of your life, according to an intricate master plan. I also know that you may not be able to see the beauty of the entire pattern until you are at some distant point.

All I can do is stand by you, a fellow weaver, and be with you in mind and spirit as you walk toward the future. All I can do is assure you that someday you will understand that it is the contrast of the dark threads to the bright threads that will make a glorious fabric when the cloth is complete.*

I love you, Mom

*Based on an Anonymous Quote

Dear Love,

The morning began with warm, spring sunlight streaming through the bathroom window. I stood at the mirror and was shocked to see the sunlight glinting off the silver strands which, almost overnight, had become entwined in my hair. As I inspected my face in the mirror, I realized that there were other apparent signs of aging which I had not really noticed before. I thought to myself, "Hmm, I am getting old looking." For a moment, a shadow of gloom fell over the sunlight in the room.

Getting older is hard for some to accept. It means roads not chosen; things not accomplished; friendships not made; and, dreams unfulfilled. Yes, there have been many things I have wanted to accomplish that I have not; roads that I have wanted to walk down but never did; certainly, a million people that I have never had a chance to develop friendships with; and, definitely a backlog of unfulfilled dreams.

However, I do not look back with passing age and regret any of my life. Instead, I am excited at looking forward into another age, the twilight of my life, with the same anticipation, faith, hope and love that I embraced in the past. I will accomplish new things; walk down roads I have always wanted to walk down; make new friendships; and, maybe, even fulfill a few of those old dreams.

And so, my silvery hairs will not be looked at as something to be ashamed of or to be banished by an artful beautician. They are reminders of how far I've come in my journey; how many things I've accomplished; how many roads I have walked; and, how many people I have known. I will wear them as badges of honor as I move into the future, because I know that I am a veteran of life.

I love you, Mom

Dear Love,

I went into the pet shop yesterday to buy some fish for my aquarium. While I was in the pet shop looking at fish, I noticed a huge aquarium of chameleons sitting in the front of the store. The pet shop owner told me that reptiles are the most sought after pet these days — chameleons in particular. I stood in front of the aquarium filled with chameleons, fascinated as they ran from area to area in their aquarium, which had been specially designed to bring out their ability to change color depending on their environment.

I never did buy any fish at the pet shop, but my visit was very worthwhile anyway. As I left, I couldn't help but muse that chameleons would be the choice of pet for this day and age. It seems that we live in a time when people are very much like chameleons — changing their looks, values, beliefs and morals, depending on the environment in which they live and work.

Now if I were to be a reptile of today, I would want to be just like the lizard, sitting by itself in the back of the pet shop in a plain tank. I would know what I was going to look like each day without having to change myself to fit the environment of the moment. My inability to change might not be exciting, but, to those people in my life, I would be predictable, and predictability means security.

I love you, Mom

Dear Love,

I was thinking about "me" today. My first reaction was thinking of "me" is a strange topic to think about first thing in the morning? Then, I thought again, "Is it really?" We should all think more about "me" once in awhile — not in an ego-centric sense, but, in the sense of taking stock of "Who 'me' is ?" and, more importantly, "Do I really like 'me'?"

After much thought, I have decided that I really like "me." I haven't done anything spectacular with my life according to our materialistic society. I'm sure that there are those who look down on me for not having worked outside the home — but — I am happy with "me" just the way I am. That doesn't mean that there aren't a few things I wouldn't like to change about "me" — a few inches off here, a few pounds off there and, maybe, four or five inches added to my height — but — these things don't count in my "me" assessment. They are my physical attributes, but they aren't the things that are going to be remembered about "me."

It is "me" — my heart, my soul and my mind — that make up the "real me" and no one and nothing can take "the real me" away from "me." That part of "me" never changes. I love "me" in my inside and I feel good that I have lived true to the values that I hold dearest to "me" — truth, honesty and, most of all, love. One of you children said it another way many years ago, when I was all dressed up to go out. "Mom, even dressed up, you are always the same." At first, I was taken aback, and then realized what a tremendous compliment it was. My children knew exactly who I was and how I would act, no matter how I was dressed or where I was going. I was "me" to them.

I love you, Mom

Dear Love,

Weekend rides into the country were a big treat when you were little. As we drove along, we would sing at the top of our lungs rounds of nonsense songs. I have forgotten most of the songs at this time. However, one line from one song sticks in my mind. It went : "...one little duck with a feather in his back, he led the others with a Quack! Quack! Quack!" I can still remember the car rocking as you screamed out "Quack! Quack! Quack!"

At that time, I was just one of the "quacking" ducklings in the car — a typical mom, just going along for the enjoyment of the day. Now, for the first time, and in the middle of my life, I find that I am the only little duck left!

I approach the challenge of being alone with an odd mixture of opposing feelings: fear — that I might not be able to find my way; and, excitement — of finding a new way, discovering a new world and myself.

I guess only time will tell what this "one, little duck with a feather in her back" will do in the future. No matter where I go or what I do, I hope, however, that I will occasionally find some little ducklings to sing raucously with me on my journey as we did long ago.

I love you, Mom

Dear Love,

Mindlessly, we enter a darkened room and flick a switch on the wall. Instantly, there is light! Never do we think of the days when light was generated only by smoky candles, oil lamps or roaring fires. Light has, without a doubt, become an unconscious expectation of life. Never do we think of the genius that invented the world of instant light — Thomas Edison.

As a youth, Thomas Edison was considered "stupid" and never expected to amount to anything by his family and peers. How wrong they were in their judgment of him! By his death, he had more than 1000 patents credited to his name, including the patent for the electric light bulb .

I remember Thomas Edison for two wonderful sayings. At his home, in Edison, New Jersey, is a sign which says something like this: Great invention is nothing more than a pile of junk and a little bit of imagination; and, second, when referred to as a genius, he made the reply that: Genius is two percent inspiration and ninety eight percent perspiration.

Thomas Edison, in these two statements, is describing principles which can be applied to any life situation. With a little bit of imagination, two percent inspiration, a lot of perspiration, a pile of junk can be turned into something great. After all, Thomas Edison lit up the whole world with these principles. Is it so impossible to think that we can light our own worlds with enough effort?

Thomas Edison didn't quit until he got it right. Maybe, we shouldn't either.

I love you, Mom

Dear Love,

A new house is being built at the end of the block on a lot which has been vacant for many years. I walked by this morning, just to see how the house-building project was progressing. It was evident from the numerous stakes in the ground that the parameters of the house had been carefully laid out. The construction crew was quite busy laying the initial foundation according to the guidelines of the stakes.

As I walked on, I thought to myself, "Setting the parameters of a house is the most basic and crucial element in the business of house-building. If this first task is not done to perfection, the rest of the house cannot be built to specifications, and the rest of the house construction can only be shoddy, making it susceptible to the first strong wind that comes along."

Building a relationship is much like building a house. Basic and crucial to beginning a new relationship is the laying out of parameters of behavior, to be used as guidelines in the actual building process.

The stakes, which mark the parameters of a relationship, are common values, ethics, morals and beliefs. Without common values, ethics, morals and beliefs, a relationship can be built, but there will be no solid foundation and no enduring structure upon completion. Just like a house, when the first, strong wind of adversity comes along, the relationship will collapse under its own weight.

I love you, Mom

Dear Love,

There is no feeling in the world like sitting in front of an open fire, whether the fire is at a campsite, deep in the forest, or right in your own living room. There is something about fires that entrances me, making me feel like curling up comfortably inside of my mind, blocking out all else except the twisting and turning of the yellow flames.

I have watched countless fires in my life. Some fires have roared with brilliant, yellow flames, shooting high toward the night sky, or threatened the house with flames, hungrily licking the fireplace walls. Huge fires are, without a doubt, more exciting and fascinating than small fires. There is an element of danger and excitement in them that keeps our attention riveted on them. Large fires, however, require a tremendous amount of fuel to keep them burning, and a constant alertness so nothing gets burned if they rage out of control. Ironically, big fires, although they create intense heat, burn out quickly.

Small fires are much more to my liking. Their flames are tiny and seem to dance on their own in various colors of iridescent blue, yellow and orange. Small fires, also, do not require much fuel to burn on for a long period of time. Maybe small fires are not as exciting as large, roaring fires, but, as I stir the ashes of my small fire, I feel the sleepy comfort that a small fire generates, knowing that it is there to warm me and not to consume me.

I love you, Mom

Dear Love,

I have stood by the seashore many times in my life — from the blackened sands of the Japanese islands, to the wild, unruly shores of the Atlantic seaboard, and the windswept beaches of the Pacific coast.

We each stand on the shore of our own unique ocean. Some of our shores are covered with coarse, black sand — as if those parts of our lives never were fully reduced to fine silt either by lack of thought or action, leaving a gritty residue underfoot. Some of our shores are littered with the rubble of life's disappointments, unresolved crises, unrequited loves, unfulfilled promises and empty dreams — like broken glass and deadly refuse buried just below the surface, inflicting pain with the tread of an unsuspecting footstep. Other shores are abundant with immaculate grains of white sand, caressed by fine, ocean mists which refresh and cleanse as if constant attention has kept the shores free from hazards that hamper our journey and harm those who walk with us.

And so, I daily walk down my own unique seashore, stopping a moment here and there, removing from among the grains of sand, bits and pieces of rubble washed up by my life and discard them, so that anyone following in my footsteps will not be hurt by anything left behind. I want the gritty residue of my mistakes to be ground into fine silt by my constant attention and energy. I want the cool, ocean mists to sweep across the shores of my life, creating a safe haven for all who wander onto them.

I love you, Mom

Dear Love,

My flight was late and so I took up a post at the edge of the terminal to watch — not planes — but people zoom from one end of the airport to the other. I thought to myself, "Where is everyone going in such a hurry? They all can't be late to make their flight? What is so important that so very few have the time to appreciate the individuals that hurry along with them?" My final thought was, "In the end of life, will all the hurrying have been worthwhile?"

Watching people scurry at the airport reminds me of the ants that scurry on the sidewalk. Under almost any park bench, there they are, hurrying back and forth, carrying things, many times too big for them, getting stepped on as they scurry along in what looks like their mindless sojourns. Yes, the people scurrying at the airport definitely look just like the ants scurrying under a park bench.

Ants or ant-people mindlessly make of life nothing more than a process to a goal and another and another ... without missing a beat. They never stop. I have decided that it is better to stand to the side of the airport terminal, and watch the people pass by, or sit on a park bench for a few moment's respite. It is here that I can smell the coffee or flowers whichever is in my vicinity.

I love you, Mom

Dear Love,

When I was a young mother, I came to believe that taking a bath, rather than being a pleasurable experience, was a torture, conceived by some diabolical, household entity. The minute, I said, "Mom is going to take a bath," a horde of little devils was let loose outside the bathroom door. Rather than being a warm, soothing, moment of peace, a bath usually meant tepid water, no privacy, hair pulling, and arguments that even Solomon could not have solved. As I'd sink into the tub, the phone was always ringing, little people were always camped out on the pink bathmat, crayon fights were going on outside the door, and the hairdryer somehow got accidentally plugged in and offered for my use in the tub. Then, of course, there was the neverending chorus of little voices asking, "Mom, when are you going to be through in there?" — as if I ever had a chance to get started.

Today, taking a bath is a totally different experience. The tub is steaming and sends goosebumps down my spine as I sink wearily into the water for a few minutes of peace. My legs and arms float contentedly on the surface of the water amongst the bubbles. There is perfect, heavenly, well-earned solitude in this watery confine. "Yes, this is the way a bath should be," I think, with total certainty.

However, I must admit, that in the back of my mind, there is maybe one, little, bubbly moment when I miss the sound of tiny voices asking, "Mom, when are you going to be through in there?"

I love you, Mom

Dear Love,

When I stand with the seawater swirling at my feet, I am reminded that we are all voyagers in this life, just like voyagers who travel the vast and wild oceans.

As I look toward the horizon, the sea is calm and tranquil one moment and voyaging on it is smooth and peaceful. However, this can change in an instant as a ferocious storm comes up, rocking the boat with erratic winds of change and turmoil.

Some of us are better sailors than others, facing the undulating tides, the capsizing waves with stalwart determination, knowing that survival means to hang on until the ocean once again returns to gentle rocking. Others are frightened and panicked by the erratic power of the turbulent sea, try to outrun the storm, and increase the likelihood of being tossed overboard and pulled under by the raging waves.

In the storms that swirl around life, harbors of sanctuary can be found for those that are lost and cast adrift, if only they were looked for. They are all around us in our friends and family. It is in the harbor of their arms that we can take shelter until such a time as the seas are calm. Perhaps, after a short respite with caring people, we can go on with renewed spirit to voyage to the four corners of life.

I love you, Mom

Dear Love,

Most people are classified according to common attributes like age, gender, race, color, creed or any number of other factors. I classify people according to the following:

— Those who dare to plunge to the deep with its uncertain perils, but its grandiose majesty; and, those who only float on the surface of life;

— Those who can see the wonder of the heavens in all its dimensions; and, those who see only the eternal blackness of night;

— Those who take time to think and wonder about the mysteries of life; and, those who live life mindlessly only for the material;

— Those who share their gifts and the depths of their souls; and, those who live like misers behind thick walls of egocentricity;

— Those for whom life is a joyous, yet, solemn celebration; and, those for whom it is no more than a passage of time.

I want to surround myself with people who plunge to the deep, are awe-struck by the heavens, who question the mysteries of life, who share the depths of their souls and find life to be a joyous celebration of each moment. These people are ageless people. They search for the truth of life, no matter how difficult the quest. It doesn't matter how else they are categorized.

I love you, Mom

Dear Love,

Struggling financially goes along with buying your first home and having a young family. I began to make all your clothes as a way of staying on a tight budget. After I tucked you in at night, I would go up to the attic under the eaves of the roof, and I would transform bright-colored fabrics into little shirts, trousers, dresses, robes, or anything else that you needed.

Sometimes, I felt bad that I could not shop in the stores for your clothes. However, even though your clothes were homemade, you were always delighted with the finished product. As I dressed you in your homemade wardrobes, I would say to myself to absolve my sad feelings, "It's not what's on their backs that count; it's what's in their hearts."

As the years went by, some of the financial pressure did ease off, but still there was not enough money to buy everyone in the family the designer label clothes that "everyone" was wearing. As a result, we would carefully shop the sale racks, discount stores and even the resale shops, looking for something that looked wonderful on you. You quickly learned that a designer label did not necessarily guarantee that a garment would look good on you or fit well. When once in awhile you would question why we could not buy all the latest fashions, I would remind you that, "It's not what's on your back that counts; it's what's in your heart."

Because your clothes were not "just like everyone else's," you became known for having a style sense all of your own and an individuality that was respected and admired. This exercise in frugality didn't seem to hurt you at all — you had friends and dates, were elected to school offices, were members of teams, and did everything every other teenager did. In fact, rather than hurt you, I believe, that not being able to buy just what everyone else was wearing, helped you develop your own self-identity, and, as a result, you became a leader — not a clone that looked and acted like everyone else.

I love you, Mom

Dear Love,

The sounds of passing trains echo through the night and I have sat by the open window and wondered many times where they are going. Thinking about those packed boxcars, I have envisioned all sorts of things inside of them. There could be animals in them headed for market. That always made me feel sad. There could be boxcars loaded with all kinds of packages and mail, bringing, not only happiness, but an equal share of sorrow to the recipients. There could be boxcars headed to factories, department stores, steel mills, and who knows where else.

My favorite boxcar, however, is the occasional one that has its door wide open and is empty. In a moment of mental abandonment, I see myself, carefully waiting by the side of the railroad tracks for the train to slow down at the next junction. I watch for the empty boxcar with the door flung wide open invitingly. As the train slows and passes, I see myself taking a few running steps, then a flying leap toward the open boxcar door as I throw my body onto the disheveled floor. As I right myself to a sitting position, I listen to the wheels clatter faster and faster with mounting excitement as they carry me in a new, unknown direction.

A crazy daydream? A wild and very dangerous thought? A mental, romantic interlude in a rather repetitious life? It just goes to show that even Moms get wanderlust from time to time before they close the window for the night.

I love you, Mom

Dear Love,

Every family has at least one of them — sometimes two of them — but without a doubt, my younger brother and I were "the ones" in my family. We were, affectionately and not so affectionately, christened, the "black sheep" in the family.

As teenagers, we were always in trouble. If we weren't supposed to do something, without a doubt, we did it. If we were supposed to do something, without a doubt, we didn't do it. I believe that the antics of my younger brother and I were the reasons why my mother was going gray and my father going bald by their mid-thirties. Life with us was a neverending series of pranks, mischief and surprises for better or worse — and — most of the time, it was worse. If we couldn't find any trouble to get into, we somehow were always in the wrong place at the wrong time. One thing to be said about having a black sheep or two in the family — life is never boring.

However, black sheep tend to tame down somewhat as they grow older. I have known many black sheep in my life, so I feel comfortable making the following generalization. One thing black sheep seem to have in common in their later years is that they tend to try and make up for some of their black sheep, youthful deeds by sticking close to the corrale when the parents they tormented are in need in their later years.

Casual spectators tend to think adult black sheep are wonderful for being there for their aging parents, but you and I know that if our parents hadn't stuck by us during our black sheep days, some of us might not be here to tell the tale.

I love you, Mom

Dear Love,

Eagles and ostriches are both classified as birds. This seems strange to me as eagles and ostriches exhibit exactly opposite characteristics. Eagles are powerful, awesome birds, ready and willing to test their wings. In no time, they are out of the nest, winging through the sky, totally aware of their environment. There isn't a leaf, a branch, or a bug that escapes their notice. With their exceptional visual acumen, they can spot their prey from high in the sky, and with great grace and dexterity instantaneously swoop down to the earth to pick up their evening meal.

Ostriches, on the other hand, are landbound from birth, clumsily breaking out of their eggs to find themselves flapping around on stunted wings. They charge around on stilt-like legs trying to take-off to the skys which never happens. Their final idiosyncrasy is that they stick their heads in the sand as if in a game of "I can't see you, so you can't see me."

If I had a choice to be a bird, I would most definitely want to be an eagle, head held high and wings powerfully spread wide, ascending and descending on the air currents, and instantaneously alert to the entire environment. I sure wouldn't want to be an ostrich with its head in the sand, pretending that because I couldn't see you, you couldn't see me.

Come to think of it, we all have the potential to be eagles or ostriches in life. Which do you want to be?

I love you, Mom

Dear Love,

I had been looking at the bush outside our kitchen window for weeks and thinking to myself, "What a sorry state it is in." The bush was overgrown with rotten limbs, dead branches and choked with vines. The leaves that had survived were at the the top, and were a lifeless color from lack of nutrient.

I decided to do something about our bush and out I went with my saw, pruners and ladder. It took me all day to saw through the rotten limbs at the bottom of the tree, clip and prune all the dead branches, tear out the choking vines, bundle them up, and drag them out to the street for pick-up.

It was an exhausting job but well worth the effort as I stood back and admired my bush. The stumps of the rotten limbs will always be there, as will the scars where dead branches were pruned away, reminders of too many years of ill-care. The remaining limbs, however, are clean and healthy looking and the leaves at the top already have taken on a sense of new life as they float in the evening breeze.

I won't know until next year if the whole bush will survive, or whether I will have to cut off more branches. One thing is for certain — pruning the dead wood off my bush has saved its life and will insure new growth. We will all have to wait now and see which limbs sprout healthy leaves and what our new bush will look like in years to come.

We should all prune periodically to insure new growth or end up in the sorry state of my bush.

I love you, Mom

Dear Love,

To be number one in school, to be at the top, to be the undeniable best — this had been my conscious ambition for as long as I could remember as a college student. College was an attempt at "straight A-ism." I studied for the sake of grades and nothing more. I never really thought about why I was trying to create this perfect academic world. Looking back, this academic perfectionism was like a tiny snowball being rolled from the top of a high hill sometime when I was young, picking up mass and speed, and creating more destruction, the farther it traveled in my life.

By the middle of my college years, the grade obsession had taken over my entire life. I viewed anything less than an "A" as a failure. I allowed myself no margin for error. I no longer studied for exams, I memorized for exams — not just pages of notes, but literally pages in textbooks. No human contact, no activity, no relationship was more important than my academic quest. Little did I ever think that in the future, I would find that this was the ultimate exercise in futility.

Did I get the A's? Yes, A's and a Summa Cum Laude degree. Was it worth it? Emphatically, no! Thirty years later, I barely remember anything I learned from my illustrious academic career, and, sadly, I barely remember anyone I went to school with. I realize now that during that period of time I was a great student, but a failure as a human being. I can honestly say, if I had to choose all over again as to whether to go for all A's and nothing else, or go for lesser grades and live a full life with the people around me, I would now choose the later.

Nobody remembers if you gradaute college with honors. Everyone remembers if you graduate life with honors.

I love you, Mom

Dear Love,

No mother and child weather the teenage years without angry words and tearful, hurtful scenes. There were many in our home during those years. There was one thing about those scenes, however, that was different than the way they may have ended in other families. No matter how ugly the scene, no matter how hurtful the words, no matter how angry the looks, I would not let the night pass without making up. It was of utmost importance to me to go to bed forgiving and forgiven.

When I was an especially rebellious teenager, I got up one morning in a terrible mood, and had a typical, angry argument with my mother. Years later, I have no idea what the argument was about but I do remember that I walked out of the house, didn't say goodbye, internally vowing that I would either never come home again, and, if I did come home, I would never speak to my mother again.

I returned home from school that day, still in a surly mood, to find the house strangely quiet. My resolve to continue the angry, silent treatment quickly faded away as I realized something was terribly wrong. My mother was nowhere in the house, odd for this time of day. Little did I know that during the day, my mother had suffered a stroke and was in the hospital. I wept inconsolably, thinking that I would never have the chance to say I was sorry and tell her how much I loved her. Life has odd little ways of reminding us of the sharp turns it can take in just a couple of hours.

As I stood by her bed in the hospital, I vowed that I never again would let a day pass without asking for forgiveness from someone I offended or forgiving someone who had offended me. I have kept that promise, as you know, as we have hugged and cried on the edge of your bed many times before you went to sleep.

I love you, Mom

Dear Love,

You are standing at the moment of second birth — the birth of adulthood. You have been stripped of all the childish things that have held you back for so many years, and you are pregnant with a million different potentialities. Just as in the experience of first birth, you are alone, naked, vulnerable, scared and crying out. A newborn adult is really no different than a newborn baby, except for size and who is responsible for parenting.

When you were firstborn, you were tiny, helpless and we were responsible for your needs and for your growth process. Now, as a newborn adult, you are big, strong and responsible for your own needs and how you grow as an adult from here on. There is a strange dichotomy in this new birth of adulthood, where you are both the parent and child simultaneously.

Once adulthood is reached, the future is totally in your hands. There is no going back to the womb of childhood where someone else is responsible for you. Being born as an adult is no less difficult than the original birth process. However, once the laboring process of youth is over, the pain should be forgotten and left behind. In its place should be, the tremendous joy that you can be whomever you want for the rest of your life. Parenting for us was a sacred and challenging responsibility. Parenting for you should be a sacred and challenging responsibility as well.

I love you, Mom

Dear Love,

Part of my maternal philosophy was that all children should learn to do puzzles as a necessary educational task. My special preference in puzzles was the wooden type that came in all kinds of pictures, and usually numbered not more than twenty-five pieces. I remember bringing them home for the first time, thinking smugly to myself, "Now, these will keep them busy for a long time!"

To my amazement, the wrappers came off with squeals of delight, the puzzle pieces were dumped on the floor, the picture was propped up as a reference guide to follow, and, within moments, the puzzles were quickly reassembled. Somehow, I had to make this a more difficult task. I removed the cover pictures so that they could no longer be associated with the puzzle pieces. This time it did take a bit longer to reassemble the puzzles — but — not much longer! I knew that I was defeated in keeping you occupied for hours, when you got the bright idea to dump the puzzle pieces from all fifteen puzzles that we owned in a huge pile on the floor. I watched in speechless amazement as you set the boards around you in an organized pattern, and reassembled all fifteen puzzles at one time from that chaotic mound of puzzle pieces.

There are times that my life looks like the puzzle pieces of those fifteen puzzles, all dumped in a heap together on the floor. Having the picture of what the puzzle should look like, would make reassembling an easy task. However, I do not know what the finished puzzle will look like in real life, so I try to remember what you did when you were little. I set the boards of my life around me in an organized manner, and I try to apply the same gleeful diligence I saw you apply to reassembling puzzles when you were little, in putting the puzzle pieces of my life together.

I love you, Mom

Dear Love,

You can tell many things about people if you take time to look at the things in their lives that normally would be considered totally insignificant. Stationery is one of those things that I believe would be considered totally insignificant. However, sometimes what is being written on says more than what is being written.

The choice of stationery tells whether you are happy or sad, busy or relaxed. Some people write on yellow legal pads; some on white bond paper; some on notes cards or postcards; some on the back of things already written on; some on perfumed stationery; some on childish stationery with large black lines; and, some on elegant engraved stationery.

My preference is bright-colored stationery. It is not really childish; it is not fancy, and, it is not expensive — but — it is expressive of a mother writing to her child away from home. It is a happy, loving way of letting you know that I am in your mailbox, the minute you open it.

I love you, Mom

Dear Love,

Grandma is ailing and it is my honor and privilege to help her get ready for bed and tuck her in at night. As I left her tonight, I wanted to run to her, the way I used to do when I was a little girl, and stay with her so that she could never leave. As she gets older, I see her fade a little bit more each day. I sense that she will not be here in the not-too-distant future. When she leaves this life, my life will be empty without her. I have been so blessed by having her as a Mother. She has been a wonderful example of wisdom, courage, perseverance and love. Following her example, has enabled me to stay true to the life I have chosen, despite the many difficulties that have arisen. Without her, I would have given up and quit a long time ago.

I am eternally grateful to her for all that she has done for me, given to me, but, most important, for all that she is — my source of inspiration. I love her more than I could ever express. The only thing I can really do for her at this stage of her life is tuck her into bed, the way she tucked me in so many times, and live out the values and principles that she taught me.

I love you, Mom

Dear Love,

"Entropy" is one of the most important words in the English language, and, yet, it is a word that is rarely ever mentioned. There are many scientific definitions for the word, entropy, but in a non-scientific sense it means that every material thing is created with a limited amount of material energy, and that energy will inevitably deteriorate over a period of time.

Rarely, as human beings, do we ever think that the process of entropy applies to us, and, yet, we are material energy, and, therefore, will someday inevitably bow to the forces of entropy — we will die. We, as the humankind, however, are gifted with another type of energy that can counteract the effects of entropy, and prepare us for the inevitability of the life cycle.

At birth, I believe, that our material energy is separated from a pure, spiritual energy source, which according to my belief, is God. At that time, we become part material energy and part spiritual energy — our body and our soul. From the very moment of birth, our material energy is involved in the entropic process. In our lifetime, however, our spiritual energy has the potential of increasing manifold times in the goodness we show toward our fellow human beings. I believe that it is in understanding the balance between the inevitable entropic forces attacking material energy, and the great potential of increasing spiritual energy that human beings can be led to a more spiritual and humane existence.

How many of us never reflect on the limits of our material energy, put everything into material things, and nothing into spiritual energy until death is upon us! Isn't it time for each of us and society as a whole, to recognize that nothing material travels with us at the moment of death; and, only the spiritual part of our lives cloak us as we make this final journey? I believe, that if we live according to this philosophy, death is not frightening, but merely a point in time when by the forces of nature, our material energy is at its lowest point and our spiritual energy should be at its highest point. Death, then, is nothing more than a gentle return to the spiritual energy or God that created us.

I love you, Mom

Dear Love,

The ocean was rough with waves crashing against the huge, blackened rocks which looked like faceless Easter Island statues, piled one on top of another. Wave after wave rolled in, covering more and more of the sand and rocks with icy froth. We walked precariously over the crevices between the rocks, consciously rejecting the danger of slipping between the cracks, or loosing our balance and falling into the watery turmoil below. The pull of the mystery of the ocean was too alluring. There was an unspoken need between us, to be as close as possible to this mysterious source of life and death, despite the dangers.

As we reached the end of the rocky climb and looked down into the ocean caverns below, there we saw a helmet-shaped, brown, ocean crab, wedged between the crevices of the lower rocks. It was being buffeted by the increasing ocean tide but the power of the tide was not enough to release it from its ocean grave. It helplessly reached out it limbs in supplication as if it was beseeching some Good Samaritan to either help it or end its misery.

Without a moments hesitation, you climbed over the rocky edge, down to the mouth of the boiling water on rocks made slippery by the growth of slimey, green algae, and struggled to save its life. Triumphantly, after keeping your balance as the ocean's, watery fingers grabbed for you, you stood with the crab, bigger than your head, in your outstretched hands.

I will never forget the sight of you arching your strong, young arms and tossing that ocean crab back to its natural home. I could see the look of triumph and pride in your eyes as you began your ascent up the rocky face of the ocean cliff. You had saved one of this earth's creatures. I couldn't help thinking of something your great-grandmother used to say — that if you save one life, you eventually save the whole world. Just think. You might have saved the ocean crab from extinction.

I love you, Mom

Dear Love,

Someday when I have a home all by myself, I want sunlight streaming through the windows making capricious patterns on my floor. I don't want shades or curtains to block my view of the treetops outside. I want the walls to be clean and stark-white, like unpainted canvas. On them, I will display the pictures I love, in odd arrangements which have meaning only in my mind, heart and soul. I want my floors to be bare and light in color with thick, soft, earthtone rugs scattered here and there — inviting people to take off their shoes and rub their toes in them.

In my home, there will be an oversized, squishy couch , inviting everyone to just flop down and sink into it. I want it to be dark in color so that people will not be afraid of getting it dirty when they curl up and go to sleep on it. There will be a plain, wood table in my home, with sturdy, comfortable chairs. It is at this table that we will all gather around and share, not only the food and drink that we have, but our laughter and tears as well.

My dogs will lie by the door and wait for me to come home, knowing that when I come home, we will enjoy our evening walk together. Walking with them, I will not be afraid because they are my friends, and, just as I have sheltered them, they will protect me.

My cats will spend their days, sleeping in the sun. When bedtime comes, they will curl up at my head and knees, purring in my ears and touching me with furry paws. They will be content knowing that I am there.

My home will be open to all, no matter what hour it is. No one will ever be turned away. I realize that I won't have much according to the material scheme of life, but, oh, how wealthy I will be in other ways!!

I love you, Mom

Dear Love,

Using the number one to designate something can mean many different things. One can mean that someone is the first to be picked for a team, or the lone one left that no one wants on their team. It can mean being at the top like the president, or a valedictorian, or it can mean being the last one, like the low man on the totem pole. It can mean being something very special as in a one-of-a-kind antique, or not so very special, as in one leftover porkchop sitting on the refrigerator shelf by itself. It can mean a little one or a big one as in one ant, one dog, one horse, one elephant, one dinosaur. It can mean a single of one kind, or when you put one and one together, one pair, which is really two but only one. And last, but not least, one can mean the beginning of something as in the first moment, or the end of something as in the last moment.

Our lives are inundated with a sense of oneness. What oneness means to me, first and foremost, is that there is only one of you — unique, special, and not like anyone else in existence. You are the one, I think of with my first thoughts in the morning, and my last thoughts each night. No other one is as important.

I love you, Mom

Dear Love,

As a baby, there wasn't anyone that gave better hugs than you did. You would climb up in my lap, wrap your short, pudgy arms around my neck, nestle your head right under my chin, and hug with all your little might. It was as if in those moments, we became one person, all wrapped up together.

As the years went by and you grew-up, you seemed to want to hug less and less. I never understood the reason why. Maybe it just wasn't something teenagers did. Maybe it seemed uncomfortable or unnecessary, but for whatever the reason, the hugs stopped. As you lost your wonderful ability to give the world's best hugs, you also seemed to loose your joy of life and ability to relate to others. I knew you were unhappy and there was little I could do to comfort you, except hug you. I became determined to resurrect in you the art of hugging that came to you so naturally as a child.

Everyday when you came in from school, I would ask for a hug. You would give me a half-hearted effort, and so I told you, I was going to teach you how to hug. You looked at me like I was crazy but I was not discouraged in the least bit. I would wrap your arms around my neck, lay your head in the crook of my chin, and in that position, I would hold you tight and hug with all my might. It took awhile, but soon you had resurrected the ability to hug and hug you did. With the ability to hug once again, you seemed to become once again a little happier, despite what was going on in your life at that time.

You have retained your wonderful ability to hug to this day, and I think about all the people you comfort and make happier with your wonderful hugs. I'm glad that we had those lessons — especially when you give me a hug.

I love you, Mom

Dear Love,

I know the last thing you wanted was to get stuck on the top bunk at school, but it does have advantages if you think about it.

In a room, when one bunk is down and one is up, the upper bunk is the only one that affords any privacy. You don't have to wake up in the morning, or go to bed at night and glance at the space above you and see the bottom of your roommate's dirty feet or tangled head of hair. In glancing from the top bunk, all there is is space. Space, when thought of correctly, can lead you any place that you want to go. You are alone up there in the top bunk, to look up and dream, with nothing except the ceiling above you. In the lower bunk, your one vision, when looking up, would be of sagging springs. The top bunk, also, allows you to have a superior status toward everyone in your room. They have to look up to you, a good position to be in, and you can choose whether to look down at them.

Maybe the upper bunk isn't so bad after all when you think of it. Maybe your perspective needs to change. So turn over and relish the thought that you have the privilege of sleeping in the top bunk — an advantage and not a disadvantage for the true philosopher of life.

I love you, Mom

Dear Love,

I have on my bed a brown teddy bear. He has a soft, little body, a round tummy, a black nose and shoe-button eyes. He was a gift from you and he is my favorite bedtime friend. I have decided that everyone should own at least one teddy bear to help them through life. The value of my teddy bear is that he is always there when I need a hug. I pick him up from the bed, wrap my arms around him, and squeeze as hard as I can — taking his breath away — that is, if he had any breath.

He reminds me so much of you when you were just a baby. There was no one that was better at hugging than you. You would get up on my shoulder and squirm around until you felt just right. It was there, molded into the curves of my body, with your head in the crook of my neck, that you would go to sleep in my arms.

I am always astonished, when I see you, that now I am the one who reaches only to your shoulder and nestles in the crook of your neck for a moment of respite, the way you did many years ago.

I love you, Mom

Dear Love,

Life is never easy. It is more like wallowing on the edge of the Sahara Desert than living in the Garden of Eden. This is one of the truths of human existence, and, yet, we, as human beings, many times, try to avoid this truth.

The secret of being successful as a human being is accepting the fact that life presents us with problems and challenges us to solve them. Ignoring problems leaves life at a standstill; actively facing problems forces growth. We can either cry, moan, or harangue at the unfairness that life hands us, or we can forge ahead, confront our problems and grow as human beings.

To deny the existence of problems is much like shoveling refuse under the carpet. In the beginning, perhaps, a little bit of refuse will only create a small lump, maybe hardly noticeable. However, as more and more refuse is shoveled under the carpet, the lump becomes bigger and everyone trying to walk on the carpet will trip on it. Also, refuse left under a carpet tends to deteriorate with time, creating quite a stench, noticeable by everyone who comes into the vicinity. Problems are no different.

It takes courage, wisdom and work to shovel out our problems. However, it is a far better to deal with them than to spend our life tripping on them, or being offended by the odor they produce.

I love you, Mom

Dear Love,

For all these years, I have been taking care of the nest, and, now, one by one, you have left it. Some of you have been reticent to leave, clinging to the side of the nest for dear life. It has taken gentle prodding to eventually get you to leave the nest and try flying on your own. Some of you have tried to leave the nest much too early. It took all my effort, to keep you in the nest, until your wings had the maturity to support you in flight. Then, there were others who just laid around the nest, not exactly fearful to leave, but not exactly interested in climbing out either. If I had allowed it, you would have been perfectly content to just lay around in the nest and exist there.

You are all out in the world flying around now — some with a little bit of encouragement, some with a little bit of coercion and some who just took to it naturally. For each of you, no matter how you began your flight, this was a giant leap into the unknown. At times, your skills have been off a little bit — soaring sometimes, nosediving at other times, and pulling up sometimes, just before you crashed — but — you have all made it.

Never forget, wherever you are, flying or soaring, even though I am alone in the nest, I am as proud as I can be at your ability to fly on your own.

I love you, Mom

Dear Love,

I know that it was hard to leave home and you are a bit homesick. In time, the homesickness will pass as you build your own home away from home. Moving on was never meant to be easy. You knew this theoretically, but the reality is overwhelming.

Don't be scared. Look at success in this current overwhelming situation in the same way you would look at having to wash a very, long, dirty hall floor at home. Just concentrate on the one, little patch of dirty floor right ahead of you. Wash that little patch to the best of your ability and when that is done, wash the next patch, then the next ... Whatever you do during this process, don't look at how much you still have to wash. Following this method, before you know it, you will have reached the end of that very, long, dirty, hall floor, and it will be all sparkling and clean. Success!

Take each obstacle you are facing now, one by one, and wash it until it is clean and sparkling — then — go onto the next. I know that you can be a success because you learned at home how to wash a very, long, dirty hall — well.

I love you, Mom

Dear Love,

It was cold in my room last night and I slipped on the old, blue cardigan that you wore during high school. It is almost threadbare at this time, but I wouldn't trade it for something new and fuzzy.

I found your old, blue cardigan while I was cleaning out the closet that used to be yours a couple of weeks ago. I put it on that night because the evening was cool and it was conveniently at hand. As I continued to clean out the closet, I realized that wearing it, made me feel warm with memories of you and all the incidences — good and bad — that made up our life together. As each memory surfaced in my mind, I knew that I was never going to get rid of this old, blue sweater.

You are gone now because you were only given to me on loan. My job as your mother was to prepare you for your place in the world, and that job is completed now. However, when the evenings are cool and I feel a moment's chill, I take your old, blue sweater out of the closet and put it on. It always makes me feel like somehow you are there, giving me a great, big, bear hug like the kind we used to share.

I love you, Mom

Dear Love,

It was the evening of the over-night, church youth group ski trip, and the weather was unbelievably warm for January in the Midwest. I was one of the chaperones for this unique outing in which forty teens would ski from 11 p.m. until 7 a.m. in the morning. Despite the threat of rain, we proceeded by bus toward the neighboring slopes, one and a half hours away.

Arriving at the ski lodge, I felt that this night was going to be a nightmare for me. Strangely enough, it was one of the most inspirational nights of my life.

On the slopes, the snow was slushy and the wind was wildly hollowing, but, nonetheless everyone was having a great time — me included. There is nothing like skiing with exuberant teens to renew one's faith in the ability of the young to adapt to the weather. However, real faith came that night while I was riding the ski lift with three young people.

During the ride up the mountain, the four of us discussed how unearthly, beautiful and peaceful it was to be riding the ski lift at three in the morning. The least philosophical member of our group reflected that riding the ski lift together was like going to church together. He was right. This was the meaning behind going to church. We rode the rest of the way to the top in reverent, companionable silence, watching the beautiful landscape pass below us. The feeling of God, community and peace — the feelings of church — were all around us. It taught me that church can be any place and at the least expected moment. It turned out to be a wonderful night and it didn't matter anymore that it had begun to rain.

I love you, Mom

Dear Love,

I had made up my mind that today would be the day that I would do all the errands that had piled up. As I backed out of the driveway, my eye caught sight of something small, brown and moving at the end of it. Screeching to a halt, I got out of the car to investigate. A small, brown sparrow lay helplessly on the driveway with a broken wing and leg, two feet from my back wheels. My first thought was just to leave it there and continue with my errands. Then, I thought, "What if a dog or a cat comes along?"

Returning to the house for a shoe box and an old wash cloth, I felt like I was eight years old again. I gently picked up the little creature, and placed it in the shoe box for transport to the Wildlife Preserve. It was a strange feeling driving along with the little, wounded bird, weakly chirping, in the seat next to me. My long list of errands seemed suddenly unimportant as we quietly road together — the strong and the weak.

The people at the Wildlife Preserve said that the small, brown sparrow did indeed have a broken wing and leg, as I suspected, and had probably fallen out of a tree. As I turned over my little friend to them, they assured me that time would heal the breaks and it would be released once more to the outdoors.

It would have been so easy to leave the small, brown sparrow lying on the driveway but I'm glad that I didn't. I didn't get anything done on my errand list, but as I left the Wildlife Preserve I felt proud and happy, knowing that my little bird would one day soar into the sky. It was the right thing to do. My list of errands will still be there another day, but there was only one chance for this little bird.

I love you, Mom

Dear Love,

I walked into your empty room tonight. Soft, gentle breezes were teasing the edge of the curtains and a wave of memories washed over me. This night was like a night long ago — the night I brought you home for the first time.

I remember looking at you — my squirming, indignant bit of humanity — as the cool night air touched your skin for the first time and the last of the evening light blinded your eyes. I remember laying you down in the crib and watching you move around until you had found a comfortable position. "What an odd position to sleep in!" I thought. I knew I could never sleep in that contorted position, and, yet, there you were, a little, sleeping ball — knees to chest, tightly sealed eyes and clenched little fists. I couldn't decide whether you looked like a baby prize-fighter, waiting to do battle with the world that would come all too soon, or, maybe just a good size roasting chicken that I could hold in the palm of my hand.

I knew at that moment that I was humbled and awe-struck by your tiny humanity. You were my priceless treasure, on loan to me, until I had to give you back to the world. And so I slipped my hand between the bars of your crib and gently nudged your hand with my finger. You stirred for a moment and reached out, curling your tiny hand around my finger. I knew instantly with that gesture that nothing would ever break the bond between us as we journeyed together.

I left your empty room tonight, still feeling your tiny hand wrapped around mine as we continue on our journey apart, but, still bound together.

I love you, Mom

Dear Love,

I was sitting outside on the hammock tonight, rejoicing in the smell of autumn. Someone was burning leaves in the neighborhood and the pungent, acrid odor permeated the air. I could hear the sound of autumn in the rustling of the drying leaves as the wind shook them in a mischievous game, just to see which one of them would fall to the ground.

To me, autumn is a contemplative season with summer beauty fading, daylight hours shortening and chilly nights descending. It is a season that reminds me of the importance of living each day. I believe that if we lived with nothing but the never-ending beauty of spring and summer, we would take it for granted and squander it without notice. It takes acknowledging that there is an end to spring and summer that reminds us to enjoy the long, warm, outdoor days, while they are here.

Likewise, it takes acknowledging and appreciating that life has a beginning and an end for us to live life to the fullest. If we don't accept this fact, until the summer beauty of our lives has faded into autumn, we risk squandering the precious days that we are given on this earth.

As I rocked in the hammock, with my hands dug deep into my pockets against the autumn chill, I thought about how fleeting life is. I pledged to myself to catch each day in my hands, like multicolored, translucent soap bubbles in the summer air, and enjoy their magic before the autumn breeze blows them away.

I love you, Mom

Dear Love,

It was cool and crisp tonight when I walked the dog — just the way a late November night should be, with a great harvest moon laying like a large pumpkin on a purple bank of clouds. One moment I was contemplating the moon, and the next moment, something darted out of the darkness toward me. I don't know who was more afraid — me, the dog or what turned out to be another dog. I put out my hand slowly so that this poor creature could sniff it and know that I wouldn't hurt it. Around his neck was a beat-up, old collar and no tags. He was either lost or had been let go to the streets to fend for himself. For a moment, he let me rub his coat and I was heartsick to feel every rib on his sides.

I tried to coax him toward the house, hoping that he would be my Thanksgiving guest, and, maybe stay permanently, but he would only come within the shadow of the door. He was too scared and too weary to get up the courage to make the final move into the house. I couldn't help thinking that someone had hurt him in the past. You could see the pain in his large, brown eyes. No one can tell me that animals don't think or feel. This forlorn creature had thought it over and decided against trusting anyone. As quickly as he appeared out of the darkness, he darted back into the shadows. I wanted to feed him and offer him a home on Thanksgiving Eve, but all I could do was leave food and water outside the door for him.

Maybe in time, he will learn to trust someone again. Like all creatures, however, trusting does not come easy to those who have been mistreated.

I love you, Mom

Dear Love,

I am a "junk" person, without a doubt. I can't resist garage sales, junk stores and resale shops. I walk down the street on the night before garbage day just to see what everyone has hauled to the curb for pick-up the next morning, hoping that I might find some cast-off treasure. I have no sentimental attachment to anything new in our house, and, yet, I am terribly attached to the things in our house that came from garage sales, junk stores and the like — things that were resurrected from the junk heap with a little bit of glue, varnish and paint.

I have come to feel that there is an almost human essence to old things that end up in garage sales, resale shops or as curbside throwaways. To me, there is a living history in them. I look at old things and I conjure up all kinds of stories about what houses they graced, what kind of people used them and what kind of secrets they could tell if they could talk.

I wish society appreciated our elderly people as much as I appreciate my old things. Our elderly people, despite the fact that they show the years of wear, have much to tell us if only we would take the time to listen. Sadly, too often, they, like my old things, are relegated to the junk heap or castoff as useless, when really they are unclaimed treasures.

I love you, Mom

Dear Love,

There is a song that I remember from my childhood that I never understood until I was an adult. It went:

"The bear went over the mountain,
the bear went over the mountain,
the bear went over the mountain to see what he could see.
And all that he could see was the other side of the mountain
and all that he could see was the other side of the mountain."

As I walked through the early stages of my life, I was much like the bear in the song. I would go from mountain to mountain, always hoping to find something exciting or special to captivate my interest and give me a reason to settle down on a particular mountain. Needless to say, I was always disappointed, as I moved from mountain to mountain because, with a cursory look before moving on, I found every mountain basically the same. None were totally blissful or perfect.

It took me well into my adult years before I realized that I was never going to find that perfect mountain, no matter how many mountains I climbed. Then, and only then, was I able to end my wanderings and choose one mountain to settle down on and call home. No place is perfect. Satisfaction and contentment comes, I discovered, when you make up your mind to give your all to the place you call home; the people you call family; and, stop wondering what could be on the other side of the mountain.

If I had understood the words, "The bear went over the mountain..." at an earlier age, I would have saved myself years of going over mountain after mountain. Wandering is for bears; people need a place to call home.

I love you, Mom

Dear Love,

Runners have always fascinated me, not only because of their power and strength, but because of their mental focus and endurance. During a race, every muscle in a runner's body is outlined as if chiseled by the sculptor's knife. Every fiber is taut and stretched beyond the endurance point, knowing that even an inch will make a difference in the outcome of the race. A runner's eyes are always myopically focused on the finish line in the distance.

I have always felt that runners are a breed unto themselves. They are supremely disciplined to take on pain and suffering in the quest for an intangible goal. That goal is not necessarily being the winner of a race, but is something that runners call a "personal best". A "personal best" means running each race better than the last race — even by a fraction of a second, without regard to the standing in comparison to the other runners. Once a personal best has been attained by a runner, another personal best becomes the next goal.

The runner's concept of a personal best would be worthwhile to adopt as a guiding principle of life. With this principle in mind, all our races in life, then, would be personal victories, no matter how small the margin of success, or how well we do in comparison to others.

I love you, Mom

Dear Love,

For countless years, I have gone through the same nightly ritual. My ritual always begins with doing the dishes; making sure the sink is squeaky clean; loading the dishwasher; and, sweeping the kitchen floor. Many years ago, I discovered that the next day would begin as a disaster if I left the kitchen a mess the night before.

The next project, I have always tackled, as part of my evening ritual, is to do the day's laundry. I think I leave the laundry until the end of the day, because by the end of the day I can only concentrate on a mindless task, and there isn't anything more mindless than doing laundry.

Taking the dog out for his nightly walk has always ended my evening ritual. Even though this task annoys me when the weather is inclement, I always feel a sense of peace and quiet walking down the streets, empty of the day's activities.

Recently, I have added a new routine to my nightly ritual. After turning off all the lights in the house and locking the doors, I turn on the small lamp facing the front window in the living room. As its soft glow fills the otherwise darkened house, I think of you, because it is for you that I leave this light on.

I love you, Mom

Dear Love,

The feeling of trust between a mother and child did not come automatically with your birth. It took years to cultivate.

The seeds of trust were planted when you were an infant, tiny and helpless. You learned that I would take care of your basic needs — to be fed, changed and comforted. The seeds began to sprout when you were a little tike, and you learned that I would always be there to help you make the transition into a life outside the home by teaching you right from wrong; the cause and effect of your actions; and, how to treat other people. Trust became firmly rooted when you were old enough to make your own decisions, and no matter what the consequences of your decisions, I remained by your side. Trust only came to full bloom, however, after years of storms between us. It was loving you unconditionally during those storms that finally allowed you to understand that I would always be there for you — you could trust me.

Cultivating your trust has taken many years for me to achieve. It is one of my most precious possessions, and I will never do anything to break that bond of trust with you.

I love you, Mom

Dear Love,

My first house was a tiny house in the mountains of northern Japan. Actually, it looked more like a concrete bunker than it did a house. It had a bathtub called a futa, that was taller than it was wide; straw mats called tatami on the floors; and, windows that slid rather than opened. There was a dirt road in front of it, and when it rained, I had to wear rubber boots to walk down the road which had turned to mud.

My second house was more civilized. It wasn't very big but had enough room for three little ones. It had a kitchen that was so small that you could cross it in one stride; one of three bedrooms that wasn't much bigger than a broom closet; and, a basement room that had the ugliest red and black carpet you could ever imagine on the floor.

Our third house was a huge, old house with a hundred years of friendly feet walking through it at night. It had a fireplace in the bedroom; a dirt basement, which you were sure was concealing monsters; and, an attic room that had once been a ballroom, to play Hide and Seek in.

Our fourth house looked like every other house on the block but it was special to me because it had an extra room that at one time had been a maid's room, which I adopted as my hideaway; a swimming pool in the backyard which constantly needed cleaning; and, a small forest of trees behind it, where everyone in the neighborhood played archeologist.

Our fifth house was bigger than it looked from the outside. It had a family room which we called the purple pit, because the furniture looked purple in there; a basement with a pool table and room enough for fifty kids; and, a homemade basketball court.

We don't live in any of these houses anymore. They have many memories attached to them, but I have learned through the years, that my real home is in your heart and you can always find me at that address.

I love you, Mom

Dear Love,

For months, the river running through the village has been choked with patches of winter ice. Within the last month, however, the snows from the north have melted, sending a flood of crystal clear water downstream. As a result, the river banks, long choked with ice, have pushed their way into the surrounding forests and fields.

As the river, once again has begun moving at a rapid rate, the river banks have become dotted with a melange of strange things. Broken tree limbs have been deposited along the banks, far from where they originally fell. All sorts of debris left by careless people bob with every movement of the water. Even an old couch has been deposited on the river bank. It will take a community effort this spring to clean-up the river bank.

However, even amongst the debris on the river bank, signs of new life are everywhere. Canadian geese are skidding on the fresh water as they come in for a landing. Ducks are beginning to give swimming lessons to their little, fuzzy ducklings. Vegetation of every sort is sprouting on every inch of the overflown banks, which only a month ago were frozen. People are casting fishing lines into the waters to see if there are any fish to be caught in this city river.

Winter comes into all our lives at one time or another, and the currents of our lives become frozen, just like the village river does during the season of winter. It would be wonderful if once a year new waters would flood our hearts, thawing the currents of our lives, pushing aside the debris accumulated during the year, and leaving behind fertile ground for new growth. It would be a worthwhile exercise for us to consciously coordinate a spring thaw in our lives with the natural spring thaw that we see all around us.

I love you, Mom

Dear Love,

Part of our heritage is French Canadian Indian. Your great-great-great grandfather came over from France to trade furs with the Black Foot Indians in the area of Canada that is now referred to as Quebec. He married a Black Foot Indian "princess", my Grandmother used to tell us. Every time the story was told, my brothers and sisters would use this piece of information as an excuse to whoop and leap around the living room, pretending that they were Indians dancing around a campfire, deep in the forest.

There really is only a tiny bit of Indian blood in me, but it is a part which has tremendously colored my life. The Indians believed that all living things were put on this earth for the aid and use of man. They believed that there are powers beyond what we, as humans, can comprehend that guide the course of our lives; that nothing happens without a purpose; and, that when something dies the spirit of that being flows into the spirit of the being responsible for its death.

I know that you are heartbroken at the accidental death of the wild horse. I believe according to the Indian part of me and you, that the spirit of that wild horse will ride with you into eternity. It will make you hold your head high — always wild and proud. It will make you run faster and harder than you ever thought possible. It will make you more sure-footed on treacherous terrain. It will make you strong, wise and capable. Once broken, it will make you able to carry others on your back.

Its life is now your destiny. It was in your path for a reason. Thank the gods of this earth for their gift to you.

I love you, Mom

Dear Love,

Legos are those brightly colored, interlocking plastic blocks that no Mother alive has not at some time scooped into boxes after her children have gone to bed; or, looked in chagrin as her vacuum has hungrily chewed up another one; or, winced in pain as she has stepped on one left behind as she makes her midnight runs. The magic of legos is that when they are locked together, they can form an almost indestructible structure — limited only by the imagination.

Legos are a child's building toy, traded in during the teenage years for another type of building material — decks of playing cards. Many times, during the teenage years, I watched in amazement at the size of the towers being built with playing cards. They reached phenomenal heights, amidst uproarious laughter, as the ever-increasing size of the tower swayed back and forth, closer and closer to disaster, with the placement of each new card.

Building a relationship is a lot like building with either legos or playing cards. The choice is up to the builder. A relationship built on shared knowledge is like building with legos — the relationship is almost indestructible, and leaves endless room for expansion. A relationship built on assumptions is like building a house of cards — the relationship is wobbly from the very beginning; sways hazardously with the addition of each new assumption; and, collapses inevitably — usually to tears, not laughter.

Building with legos lacks the element of excitement that building with cards does, because with the placement of each interlocking lego, you are sure that your structure will stand. However, completing a structure built of legos leaves a feeling of accomplishment; trying to build a structure with cards inevitably leaves a mess which someone sooner or later has to pick up.

I love you, Mom

Dear Love,

The Sunday newspaper was crammed full of ads selling everything under the sun for unbelievable prices, typical of January. However, the ads that caught my interest were the ones selling whole rooms of furniture. In some of the ads, you could buy bedroom sets, dining room sets or living room sets, all with coordinated pieces. Some of the ads went one step further — not only could you purchase an entire set of matched furniture, but you could also buy every accessory shown in the ad, eliminating the need to shop for pictures, vases, statues, flowers or anything else for the particular room purchased.

I giggled to myself, as I closed the paper, and looked around at the way my home is decorated. There is absolutely nothing in any room bought in room settings, much less with complete accessories. No two pieces of my furniture match in color or style. Most of my furniture was bought in garage sales, or resale shops or were hand-me-downs from generous friends. As far as accessories, just about every accessory I own, from pictures to flowers, has a history behind how I came to own it, who gave it to me, and why it has a special meaning to me.

I could never conceive of buying a whole room full of furniture and accessories at one time — just to fill up a room. For me, the only way to decorate a home is to fill it with things that have meaning, making of it a temple filled with sacred reminders of the people I love.

I love you, Mom

Dear Love,

Thirty years ago, as a young woman with no children, I had a wonderful job in the infant field of computer science. Everyone knew me as a computer whiz in my office. I wrote manuals, worked bugs out of ornery programs and designed whole office systems. There was no problem that I could not solve, and there was no one in my office that did not rely on my expertise. However, when you children came along, I chose to leave the computer field and devote myself to a new career — motherhood.

I remember returning to the office several years after I had resigned to be a full-time mother. I was shocked by the fact that all the systems I had designed and implemented, only several years before, had already been replaced; all the manuals I had carefully written were now obsolete; and, there were hardly any familiar faces among the office employees. As I left the office, I said to myself, "So much for career immortality!"

I couldn't wait to return home after my sojourn back into the business world. I hugged you all close to me for a long time. Sitting there with you in my arms, I knew, without a doubt, that I had made the right choice by giving up my computer career for a mothering career. My mothering job would never be obsolete, like the systems, manuals and programs I had worked so hard on at the office. It was clear to me that day, that you were my only chance in this life to gain a bit of immortality. With this new insight, I was more determined than ever to do the best job that I could as your mother.

I love you, Mom

Dear Love,

My sister's dog, Emmy Lou, is of the rottweiler breed. She stands about waist high, has a big head, huge teeth and is as strong as an ox. Walking Emmy Lou down the street brings frightened looks from everyone, and they pass as far away from her as possible. I am always amazed at this reaction to her because, despite her size, ferocious looks, and obvious strength, she wouldn't hurt a flea. When she came to live with me, I had thought to myself, "Now, here is the perfect watchdog." I learned quickly that the most Emmy Lou would do if a robber entered the house is smother him with kisses. So much for my organic security system.

Emmy Lou is frightening to adults, but strangely enough, children are undaunted by her. They run right up to her and put their arms around her neck, and, then, of course, she rolls over to have her tummy scratched. Fear is something that children are taught. What Emmy Lou looks like, is not what Emmy Lou is at heart. I only wish that people would judge Emmy Lou for what she is, not for what she looks like, or on preconceived notions of what rottweilers are supposed to be.

The principle of fear that is applied to Emmy Lou is the same principal that is sadly applied to many people who look different. Just think of how many opportunities are missed to make good friends, just because someone looks different or has been prejudged by others. We all need to take the chance and get beyond looks and preconceived notions. Just think of Emmy Lou. Underneath the ferocious looks, she has a heart as big as her head and the temperament of a pussy cat — just the right combination for a faithful companion.

I love you, Mom

Dear Love,

The day was typical of early fall with warm, dry air filtering through the screen door. The mail was late that day, and I went to pick it up from the front porch just at the time school was letting out. As I grabbed the mail, I saw two young boys and a girl huddled on the sidewalk at the end of our driveway. They weren't more than ten or eleven, were well-dressed and carried school bags. As I turned away to go back inside the house, I heard a young voice cry with glee, "Poke it again!" With those words, I was instantly alert. I calmly put the mail down and walked down the stairs to see what was going on. As I came down the walk, the three children scattered in all directions as fast as they could. I walked over to where they had been squatting in a huddle. To my horror, a small, brown bird lay in a bloody, pathetic, little ball in the middle of the sidewalk at the end of the driveway. These children had been poking sticks into it as it lay there hurt and dying.

Rage welled inside of me, as I picked up this tiny, now dead, creature. I buried it in the backyard so that it would have one shred of dignity in its death. I sat morosely for awhile on the porch steps and thought about those children who looked like everyone's children. Will their cruelty grow as they grow? Will they continue to poke sticks into other defenseless animals? Or will they progress to poking cruel words and deeds into the wounds of people they judge as defenseless? Bullies are really small, insidious people who only pick on those whom they deem weaker than they are and they always run when they are caught. They are the dregs of humanity, no matter how old they are.

I love you, Mom

Dear Love,

She stood in the spotlight of the auditorium. She would give the valedictorian's address this year. A warm smile lit her face. Her curly hair was pulled back and held demurely in place by a white ribbon. Her classmates stood in ovation as she rose to give her speech.

She began her speech a little too fast in the beginning — obviously in order to control her rampant emotions — but she slowed to a normal measure quickly and spoke from her heart. She said to her classmates that they were all crossing a threshold, stepping into an unknown region. That unknown region was the adult world. There would be much pain in this transition, but pain was essential if one was to grow. She continued by saying that the painful situations in life must be faced with courage and honest appreciation of the facts; then, and only then, would wisdom, strength and integrity grow. She closed by saying that to run from the pain of life was to forfeit adulthood and remain a child forever.

These were very deep words from a young woman. I hope that her fellow graduates, as well as the adults in the audience, took them to heart. I know that I did.

I love you, Mom

Dear Love,

We called my grandmother by the name "Mimmie." The name "Mimmie", I learned as I grew older, was a distortion of the French word "Mimmir" meaning "mother." My grandmother was French Canadian and part Black Foot Indian. Mimmie was, to say the least, a tough little lady. There wasn't a thing that she set her mind to do that she did not do to perfection. Because she was this way, she expected everyone else to be this way as well. In our house, "Mimmie's word" was law and God help the person that crossed her.

I didn't learn much from her growing up, despite her authoritarian rule, but I learned an invaluable lesson from her during her last years of life. Over a period of almost ten years, she suffered mini-strokes, leaving her more and more debilitated, until she was totally incapacitated and bedridden. During those final years, as I helped care for her, dragging my little children along, I realized that the greatest gift she gave to me in life was the opportunity to teach my children the meaning of the word "compassion." Without victims like Mimmie to take care of, there is no opportunity to learn what compassion really means. Without an understanding of what compassion means, we all run the risk of being discarded should we ever be in the position of being victims.

I love you, Mom

Dear Love,

Baseball is considered the all-American sport. Life in many American homes during the spring and summer of every year is centered around little league baseball practice and game schedules hung on the refrigerator door. Our home was no different.

A number of years ago, two young men were playing baseball together on a little league team in the neighborhood. Both young men were extremely dedicated to their team, and put their all into practices and games. All season long their statistics were neck to neck — one week one would be ahead, and the next week, the other would be ahead. It was obvious that picking a member for the all-star team was going to be a difficult task for the coaches that year.

The day after the announcement was made, the young man who won the spot on the all-star team, showed up at our door, looking for you. This was unusual because even though you and he were teammates, you didn't hang around together or even go to school together. He stood awkwardly in the doorway, waiting for you to come to the door. When you came down the stairs, he shook your hand, and told you, that he was giving you his position on the all-star team. His reason was that he felt you had played better than he had this year, and that he was only given the spot on the all-star team over you because he was the coach's son. You were thrilled.

It really didn't matter who was the best player on that little league team that year. All I know is that, in my eyes, the all-American game of baseball never had a greater hero than that young man that stood in my doorway that hot summer afternoon and gave up his place on the all-star team to you, my son.

I love you, Mom

Dear Love,

Flowers arrive in floral shops across the city in large, dirty, white, cardboard boxes. No matter how many times a shipment of flowers is opened, there is always an intake of breath as the layers of cheap, shredded paper are peeled away, and sleeping stalks of every imaginable shape, texture and color are exposed. Gently, each stem is lifted from its nesting place and the dead foliage is trimmed away. A sharp cut at the bottom of the stem completes the cleaning process and the stem is plunged into a bucket of warm water.

All fresh flowers have one thing in common, despite their vast array of different characteristics. Their petals are curled in tight, little balls — one petal entwined around and over another petal, as if by winding themselves together, they are in some way preserving their lives for the journey to the store. No matter how gentle one might be or how sophisticated ones' tools might be, the petals of each flower cannot be opened prematurely. They will unfold, petal by petal, imperceptible to the human eye, according to their own timetable. To attempt to pry the petals open will only destroy the beauty within each bud, leaving behind broken, bruised and dying shreds of vegetation.

I have learned to be patient, sitting with my buckets of brightly colored buds all around me. I know that in time, with gentle hands and warm water, the petals will unfold, and, then, and only then, will their beauty be released for all to see.

Many of life's situations are like these flowers. Sometimes those situations that seem most likely to bloom never do, and some that seem the least likely, blossom gloriously. To succumb to the temptation, however, of forcing life's situation to bloom prematurely, is to run the risk of destroying the possible beauty that with care and time will bloom on its own.

I love you, Mom

Dear Love,

How many times when you were little did we hear the words - It's a bird! It's a plane! It's SUPERMAN! I don't think that there is hardly anyone alive that doesn't know the name of the man dressed in a bright blue suit and sporting a red cape, who zooms across the sky to the rescue of someone in distress.

The Superman, I saw this evening, looked a lot like one of the great superman actors of all times, but this man was literally encased in wheelchair, unable to breath on his own, unable to move anything but his head and neck.

Christopher Reeves is a victim of a spinal cord injury and is paralyzed from the neck down. He will never play the role of Superman again in the movies. And, yet, as I watched him tonight, I couldn't help thinking that in many ways he is more a superman in his disability than he ever was when he had the ability to leap tall buildings and save damsels in distress. I listened to him speak, and he said words that I will never forget and should never be forgotten. He said that he has learned that the body is not you, that the mind and the spirit are who you really are.

How often we worry about the little things in life — an extra pound here or there, a spot of acne on our face. Do we ever think that there is a possibility that all of human movement might be taken away, and we would be left like, Christopher Reeves, unable to perform even the most simple of human functions? Christopher Reeves, as superman could scale tall buildings in a single bound, but to me, he has become a real superman with the boundless spirit he exudes from his wheelchair.

I love you, Mom

Dear Love,

There are two identical houses, sitting side by side on our block — identical, that is, until several weeks ago when one of the houses was surrounded by a beautiful, black, iron-wrought fence, six feet in height. Walking down the street the other day, I was musing about these two houses. The house with the new fence has an absolutely breathtaking garden and grass worthy of a putting green. It looks elegant, quiet, lovely — almost as if no one lives there. The house without the fence has a yard, where the grass is matted down like a well-worn carpet, dandelions in abundance and is studded with a colorful assortment of play equipment, balls, buckets, bikes of every size and shape. In sharp contrast to the fenced house, this yard is constantly filled with people and sounds of laughter reach out to the front walk.

Looks are great but not at the price of excluding people from the landscape. One yard is like a beautiful still life painting; the other is a movie picture and the sights and sounds are music to my ears.

I love you, Mom

Dear Love,

You were in second grade and your brother was in kindergarten. Normally, you were best of friends, but for some particular reason on this fall afternoon, the two of you were battling to the death outside the kitchen door. I don't know why you were mad at him, and, I'm sure, you don't remember at this point either, but you were as mad as a wet hen.

You were both called in to explain what the commotion was about. What the argument was about was probably trivial but using the "F" word while arguing, I did not feel was trivial at all. This was just not acceptable language in our house. Your defense was that you had learned the word on the playground and "Everyone uses it." My mother would have washed my mouth out with soap had I been the offender. However, I wanted to really make an impression on you. Your punishment was not being able to attend your friend's birthday party that Saturday. The reason: if you talked that way right outside of our back door, you couldn't be trusted not to talk that way at your friend's birthday party. You were angry at me all week and there were times I felt like giving in, canceling the punishment and letting you go. I didn't, however, and you survived not attending the party. Needless to say, you never used that word again or gave the excuse that "Everyone uses it."

I love you, Mom

Dear Love,

Bike riding is my favorite form of exercise. There is no feeling in the world, that makes you feel younger, than riding a bike with the wind in your face as you automatically pedal mile after mile.

On my bike rides, I ride at an easy pace — fast enough to get exercise and slow enough to notice the world around me. However, there are two groups of riders that drive me crazy on the bike trail: those who ride on the hardest gear and those who ride at top speed.

Those people, who ride their bikes on the hardest gear are convinced that they are getting the best cardiovascular exercise, despite the fact that studies have shown, it is the number of rotations, not the force of rotations, that make the cardiovascular difference. People, who are out on the bike trail purely for the exercise, and not for the pleasure, tend to ride myopically. They concentrate on the road ahead of them, never looking right or left, just ahead, driven in a sense toward some imaginary goal. I always let bike riders like this zoom by me, and, I wonder, if they are as driven in life as they are driven on the bike trail.

There are also those bike riders who ride at top speed, having the same possessed look as those that ride their bikes on the hardest gear. They are hunched over their handle bars like turtles with peddling legs. They, too, never look right or left, just ahead and down the road, to get where they are going as fast as they can. They weave in and out of everyone else on the bike trail, as if the devil himself is after them.

I often feel sorry for these two groups of riders because they seem so joyless in their pursuit. I often wonder if they ever take notice of anyone or anything on the trail. I bet they are the same people that I see in cars, honking impatiently, weaving in and out between cars, disgusted and chagrined because traffic doesn't move quick enough for them. I must admit, that I always get some malicious delight out of catching up with them, either on the bike trail or in a lane of traffic.

I love you, Mom

Dear Love,

Mary Shelley's book, "Frankenstein", should be required reading for all people. Young Dr. Frankenstein was brilliant and driven to achieve that which to this day is beyond the human realm — the resurrection of life. In his quest, he did create life but not of the humankind. In the end of the story, Dr. Frankenstein tries to run from the monster that he created and destroys all those he loved. Who really was the monster in this classic tale? Frankenstein with his misshapen body or Dr. Frankenstein with his misshapen sense of ego?

There is a bit of Frankenstein in all of us. We become monsters and create monstrous situations when we place ourselves above the laws that govern society and the humankind. When we run from the monsters we create, instead of facing the consequences of our decisions, we usually destroy the people we love the most, just like Dr. Frankenstein.

I love you, Mom

Dear Love,

As a little girl, I couldn't sleep in a room with any light at all. Light in the room meant shadows leaping off the wall at me and I was afraid of them. I would lie in bed at night with the blankets pulled over my head. Periodically, I would get the courage to lift the blankets and peak out. To my horror, there would always be this big, lumpy shape looming over me on the wall. I would then quickly huddle under the blankets, hoping the big, lumpy shape would not discover me. It took many years for me to realize that the shadows on the wall were the reflections of my own behavior. I was creating this big, lumpy shape every time I lifted the covers and peaked out.

Coming to this realization also taught me something about my life. When I cower under the bed covers of my mind because there are monstrous problems facing me, and peak out only periodically, my problems always become monsters on the walls of my life. The sooner I throw off the covers of my mind and face what seem to be monstrous problems in full light, the sooner I am able to sleep in peace.

I love you, Mom

Dear Love,

Grandma gave me a beautiful crystal vase many years ago. It was intricately cut and when you held it up to the light, different colors could be seen in the facets.

Twice a year, I go through the ritual of washing everything in the house. Yesterday, as I was rushing to get the job done, I took my precious vase, along with three or four other things out of the china cabinet, and headed for the sink with them. In my haste, I lost my grip on the beautiful crystal vase that Grandma had given me, and to my horror, it fell to the floor and shattered in a million pieces. There would be no way that it ever could be put together again. All I could do was take the broom, sweep up the shattered pieces and throw them into the garbage.

Trust is much the same as Grandma's crystal vase. When it is shattered, due to carelessness or thoughtlessness, it becomes an irreparable mess. Trust, however, need not end up in the garbage like grandma's vase. It can be melted down with the hot fires of honesty and humility, and, hopefully, something new molded from the shattered pieces.

I love you, Mom

Dear Love,

Columbus Park was the neighborhood hang-out when I was a little girl. It had a wonderful playground with swings that we spent countless hours on; bushes to play hide-and-seek in; an archery range which we didn't dare go near; and, best of all, a huge pond complete with boathouse and boats. It was a spectacular place to have fun and play in those days.

I drove by Columbus Park on my way home from the city the other day, and I pulled into the boat house parking lot just for a minute. The boat house is boarded up and decrepit, and probably has not been used for many years. The grounds are knee-deep in litter and garbage. The pond, instead of being crystal clear, like I remember, is slimey green.

The condition of the pond upset me the most. As children we used to play in that pond to cool-off. By the time we walked home, our clothes would be dry, and no one ever knew we had been wading in the pond. If you went for a dip in the pond today, you would come up green and slimey.

As I pulled out of the parking lot, I kept thinking to myself that if we swim innocently in clean water, we drip dry and no one is the wiser. However, if we swim in a slimey pond, we come up smelling and looking like pond scum and there is no way of covering the smell or the look. How many of us forget that when we are swimming around in life.

I love you, Mom

Dear Love,

Raising children is probably one of the most difficult jobs in the entire world. Dealing with little people is aggravating and exasperating many times. Probably, the most exasperating thing I had to deal with as a mother of little children is when one of you would fall to the floor and have a temper tantrum. You would wail and scream, cry and yell, kick your feet up and down and pound your fists on the floor — hoping that eventually you would get what you wanted. You learned quickly that this was not going to have the desired effect, and, in fact, worked in the reverse. As a result, you soon stopped having temper tantrums and resorted to other tactics to wear down my motherly resolve when you wanted something.

I find it amazing that the world is populated with adults that exhibit this infantile capacity to have temper tantrums. They don't get on the floor and kick, but they are the people around us, who are always finding excuses for the problems they create or yell and scream when they have to pay for inappropriate behavior. They are the adults that never thought they would get caught or find a million reasons to pass the blame to someone else.

Hey, adults of the world — it is time to get off the floor and realize that this behavior is appropriate only for anyone under three — well, maybe two.

I love you, Mom

Dear Love,

We went shopping last evening for something, which until this time had never been a part of your wardrobe — the power suit. It doesn't seem to be that long ago that you were dangling your chubby, little legs off the bed, while I was trying to squish all your toes into tiny tennis shoes with fluorescent letters on them. It doesn't seem that long ago when you were struggling with clumsy fingers to follow my directions on how to tie your shoelaces or when suddenly your gym shoes were bigger than mine, laces untied and trailing behind you.

Today, you are in a subdued, dark-colored suit. Your unruly hair is pulled back conservatively. There is a slight scowl on your mouth as you turn and look at this new person standing in front of the mirror. You inspected yourself from every angle — shocked at the person you were seeing.

You are all grown-up and looked wonderful as you came down the stairs to grab the car keys and head for your first job interview. It was like seeing a butterfly emerge from a two decade cocoon. Very seriously, you said to me as you left, "I look so old." patting a stray hair in place. "You look so old," I thought to myself, "and I feel so old."

In my heart,I wished you good luck. I don't feel that you needed the power suit but you certainly did look the part. Your fresh youth and sparkling personality will carry you wherever you want to go, I'm sure.

I love you, Mom

Dear Love,

Labels, labels, labels — we live in the age of labels — labels on socks, pants, shirts, hats, gloves, on everything imaginable. Labels are a sign of status to many people. The presence of labels can make you an insider or an outsider, cool or a nerd.

We had been out shopping for most of the day, trying to find just the right pair of blue jeans. In the tenth store we visited, you found on the sale rack, a pair of blue jeans that were the current rage — with one very large flaw — the designer label had been intentionally cut off the back, probably to sew on another pair of jeans. It was a sad commentary on the American obsession with labels and you and I had a good laugh about it. You bought those jeans for practically nothing, minus the label, came home and painted a mock designer label on the bare spot where the label should have been. We laughed at your workmanship and the statement you were making about "label mentality."

I have often wondered why other people's name on our clothes is so very important, when everyone has a perfectly good name. Does having the right label on our clothes, make us smarter, more attractive, kinder — or — does it really show that we are lacking in self-confidence and self-esteem? The bottom line is this — do clothes make the person or does the person make the clothes? I think I will stick with my own name.

I love you, Mom

Dear Love,

Halloween has always been my least favorite childhood event. Weeks before this nightmare occasion, I would sit at the sewing machine half the night, making costumes to transform you into superman, a princess, a witch or whatever else was the current rage of the day. You couldn't wait to dress up and wear this costume which would transform you into another person for one whole day and night. I just couldn't wait until it was over for another year.

Walking through the neighborhood with you trick-or-treating, gave me an opportunity to think about the masks that we wear every day. How many of us wear different masks, depending on who we are with and what we are doing — one with our children, one with our husband or special someone, one with the people at the office and so on. We wear these masks because we are afraid to expose our real selves. Some of us get so caught up in the mask routine that we have no idea who the real self is.

Peeling off the masks, that we use to cover the real self, can be a very painful process. It requires delicate, psychic surgery with a great deal of honesty. It is a worthwhile endeavor, however, because it is much easier to breath as a human being, wearing no mask at all.

Although it is fun to run around for a day and night of madness wearing a mask and pretending to be superman or spiderwoman; it is not much fun on a daily basis. Halloween, once a year, is plenty in my book.

I love you, Mom

Dear Love,

I have never told this to anyone and it needs to be said. You were about three. I don't know what the particular incident was, but as all parents get at times, I was upset and frustrated with the work and responsibility of raising little children. I was angry at you because you were not doing whatever it is that I asked you to do. I remember yelling at you and reducing you to a huddled, frightened mass. To make matters worse, I shoved you, none too gently, into the hall closet.

You were only in there several moments, before I rushed down the front stairs, threw the door open and grabbed you sobbing in my arms. Over and over again, I said, "I love you and I am sorry for doing this to you." I sobbed so hard, that despite your own tears and fears, you tried to comfort me by saying, "Don't cry, Mommy. It's alright." No, little one, it was not alright and I will never forget this scene as long as I live. Holding you in my arms, I vowed that I would never do anything like this again. I will always be sorry for that one incident. Please forgive me.

I love you, Mom

Dear Love,

It is so difficult to be "a Mom" at times. In many ways, Mom is an innocuous word, describing not who I am as a person, but rather the accumulation of the many things that I do.

Who is your mother? I am a person with needs and wants like any other person, who has chosen to sublimate them to the needs and wants of those in my care. I have hopes and dreams for a future just as "me" — things that I want to do, people I want to see, experiences I want to be involved in — that I have had no reason to share with anyone. As a person, I go far beyond the piles of laundry I wash and clothes I iron; beyond the beds I make and the floors I scrub; beyond the endless grocery shopping and cooking I do; and, the rides I give. In my mind sometimes, I live in fairytale places, wear pretty clothes, and I am fussed over by everyone around me. When I come back to the reality of just being your Mom, I know, however, with my whole heart that there is no other place I would want to be.

My title as "your Mom" will far surpass any title that I would have ever achieved out in the world. It does have its drawbacks at times, but, if I had to choose it all over again, I would never want anything more than to be your mother.

I love you, Mom

Dear Love,

Satan is alive and well and he came to my door today on Halloween. He was all dressed up in bright red satin, carried a rubber pitchfork and had the largest black satin cape one could ever imagine. His cherubic face didn't quite match the image he was trying to portray.

The subject of whether Satan or the devil is alive today is not a matter for small talk in a society which has adopted the moral approach that anything goes as long as "I get what I want." I, myself, believe that Satan, not only is alive and well today, but is actively involved all around us.

Satan is out there in school yards where the quietest kids, or the smartest kids or the kids that seem different, are ridiculed and mocked and not allowed to be part of a normal school existence. He is out there in marriages when husbands or wives cheat on each other and pass it off because "Everyone is doing it." He is in homes, where physical and emotional abuse is the norm, when a hit to the head is considered "just a little love tap," and insulting remarks or namecalling are considered "just teasing." He is out there in business when unethical means are used to achieve unfair gains. He is out there in any situation where there is a cold, calculated, disregard of the rights of others, or the physical, emotional or spiritual existence of any human being is demeaned or destroyed.

Satan is alive, well and working very hard these days. He doesn't wear red and black satin clothes. He looks just like any of us, wearing jeans or sweats, a business suit or dress and carrying a school bag, a purse or a briefcase. I, myself, like the red and black satin version of Satan better than the modern version. He is much easier to spot in a crowd.

I love you, Mom

Dear Love,

The sores and scars on my face and body have been accumulating for many years. As a child with a skin disease, the neighborhood children taunted me with cries of "leprosy" and "elephant hide." As an adult with cancer, people tended to wonder what is wrong with me.

I have developed a philosophy over the years about these sores and scars, that I would like to pass on to you. They are a reminder every day, when I look in the mirror, that I am mortal, that someday I will die. However, even though it is a jolting thought, it is not a gloomy thought anymore. Looking at these sores and scars and what they are symptoms of, has made me very realistic about life — it is short, should be lived with great reverence and not wasted.

I accept the fact that I have no control over the scars and sores that form on my face and body, but, I realize, I am in total control of the scars and sores I leave on my own life and the lives of those around me.

I love you, Mom

Dear Love,

The time was just around noon and my favorite Soap Opera was going to start any minute. You were all pre-schoolers, sitting around the table and munching on peanut butter and jelly sandwiches. Of course, I was totally engrossed in the latest escapades of the dashing stars on the television and not paying any attention to you. Out of the clear blue, a little voice said, "Wasn't Susan married to Bob? And why is she sleeping in the same bed with Alan?" That question changed the routine in our house forever.

It had never dawned on me, that by watching the soaps during your lunch hour, I was teaching you at a preschool age about abuse, adultery, divorce, cruelty, cheating, lying and a myriad of other things, so against the principles that I believed in. Therefore, on that fateful day, with a flick of my wrist, the television was clicked off for the majority of your childhood. The new ruling: There would be no television in our home, except for any program with educational value, which we would watch as a family.

As a result, homework was completed, books were read, puzzles were put together, pictures were drawn, plays were written and performed and dinner was never held up for a television program. I know that you weren't considered as cool as your classmates, who watched every sitcom on television, but because of this ruling, you learned to be communicative, creative and your sense of ethics and morals were developed around the kitchen table with me, rather than around the television with the latest soap opera star. Some people thought I was crazy, but, in actuality, the decision to make the television a reward in our home rather than a right, was the smartest decision I ever made as a mother.

I laughed the other day when you emphatically stated that "Your children were not going to watch television at home just like you couldn't." I guess over the long haul, I really wasn't the meanest mother on the block.

I love you, Mom

Dear Love,

Since I was very young, I have had what I will call "a sense of mission". By this phrase, I mean, that I have felt that I was to do something, be something, accomplish something — but — I have never known for sure exactly what my mission was to be. I had the brains to be just about anything I wanted to be, but I have only pursued higher education in my later years. I had the determination to move mountains if I wanted to, but my life has really been nothing but a series of molehills. I had the opportunity to develop a career which would have made me very rich and very professional, but I chose to be a mother.

This sense of mission has troubled me many times over the years. I did not do anything that accumulated material wealth. I spent my time at odd jobs so that I could be home with you and be involved in your life. I did not become famous and find a cure for anything in particular; I spent my time nursing you through colds, flu and sometimes just the blues. I did not pursue an advanced degree; but read storybooks to you and tucked you in every night. I did not use the opportunity to develop a professional career; it always seemed more important that you have someone there after school.

I guess to many women and men of my age, I am a dismal failure and have really done nothing with my life. However, as I see you all bloom as adults, I am beginning to realize that being a mother was my mission in life. In being there for you in life — nurturing you, caring for you and loving you — I had the awesome responsibility of developing for the next generation, fine, young people.

You and all those I have touched, through being involved with your life, will be my immortality. What I have done with my life will live long after material wealth is gone and professional achievements are obsolete. The time and effort put into children is never obsolete but keeps growing, long after the parenting job is over.

I make no apologies. My mission was to be your mother and there isn't a better profession in the world.

I love you, Mom

Dear Love,

Sitting in the family room is a very large, ivy plant. Up until yesterday morning, it was covered with beautiful, green foliage. This morning, however, I awoke to find that the family room floor was covered with somewhat sickly-looking green leaves. Obviously, my new kitten had attacked it during the night and left the mess for me. As I swept up the mess and cut back the naked stems to the roots, I wasn't too dismayed. I knew that this ivy plant had good solid roots and would be growing more beautiful foliage in no time at all — that is — if I could keep it out of the reach of my kitten.

Self-esteem is much like my ivy plant. If the roots are well-developed and solid, no matter how much unjust criticism, blame, and accusation tear away at us, self-esteem, rooted way below the surface of our personality, will eventually re- grow to cover our naked and hurting spirit.

The initial planting process is done by parents and it is their responsibility to plant the seeds of self-esteem deep in the soul and tend them carefully until maturity. If self-esteem is rooted deeply, the cruelty of the world may harm the outer leaves, but the plant will re-bloom, stronger and more beautiful than before.

I love you, Mom

Dear Love,

God and I have had such a very, unique relationship. I believe in Him with every breath I take; with every time I look in wonder at a new baby; or, marvel at the complexity of the heavens and the earth. It is the order in the universe that totally convinces me of the existence of a Divine Being. However, despite my total belief, I cannot picture God, as I know others can. I only see Him with my heart. I know He is merciful beyond any concept of mercy. I know that He is love beyond any concept of love. I know that He is compassionate, understanding and forgiving. I believe that He gave me the gift of life, and, that someday, I will have to give Him back the spiritual essence of it.

Maybe it is just as well, that I cannot focus on some visual image of the Almighty Creator, because if I was focused on His image, I would miss the godliness when you reach out your hand to comfort me, when you put your arm around me and when you tell me that you love me.

It is through the look in your eyes that I find the one vision of God that I have and that is your love.

I love you, Mom

Dear Love,

As a child, when I was upset about something or needed a quiet place to go, I used to walk to the neighborhood church. There was something tremendously calming about sitting in the back of church. I would sit there and talk in my mind to God, just the way I would talk to another human being. As I left the church after minutes or an hour, I always had a great sense of peace.

As a young mother, church doors had become locked during the day, so I no longer was able to find respite in the back of church. I found, however, that talking with God did not necessarily mean that it had to be in His sanctuary. As strange as it sounds, I found one of the best places for me to pray was at the ironing board. It was in the stillness of the basement, with the iron whisking back and forth, that I would talk with my Creator and let Him help me press out the wrinkles of my mind and heart.

I love you, Mom

Dear Love,

Going to Riverview Amusement Park was an adventure that my whole family looked forward to each summer. We would spend the entire day riding all the rides, playing all the games and eating as much junk food as we could possibly consume. I was never one that could stomach the rides, especially roller coasters, so I had to find things that were ground level and wouldn't make me sick.

Because of my queasy stomach, one of my favorite spots at Riverview, was the large haunted house. It was one place were I could go and have fun without dealing with the motion sickness that plagued me. After a few years, I knew every inch of the Haunted House, except for the Room of Mirrors.

The Room of Mirrors was a maze of mirrored doors. You were not able to just walk in and find the door that opened to the next part of the maze. As I would go from one door to another, a sense of claustrophobia would arise in me and a feeling of panic that I wouldn't find the door that would let me out. I clearly remember the feeling of relief, when I finally worked through the maze.

There are times even now in my life, when I feel that I am back in Riverview in the Hall of Mirrors. Panic rises in me because I can't find the right door to let me out. Riverview taught me a good lesson for life, however. There is always one unfound door, somewhere in the maze, that will let you out, even though it takes opening every door.

I love you, Mom

Dear Love,

I remember very little from my college days. There is, however, one concept that I learned in Philosophy class that is still as vivid in my mind today as it was thirty years ago. Paraphrased it goes something like this — unconditional love exists when the physical, emotional and spiritual well-being of another person is more important to you than your own (Father John Powell).

While you were growing up, unconditional love meant that as a parent it was the good of the "we" over the good of "me". It meant loving, despite any recognition, reward or sometimes even love returned. It meant that you could hate me and I still loved you. It meant wanting nothing from you — not time, not money, not security in the future. It meant being happy when the day came that you had a life of your own.

Today, unconditional love means that I love you with or without your presence in my life. I love you no matter how many miles and months separate us. I love you not for what you achieve, for what you become, but just because you exist. It means I will love you for all eternity — with no conditions, no strings attached.

In a world filled with conditions, this concept is powerful stuff to remember.

I love you, Mom

Dear Love,

Attending the circus was a yearly event in our household. Everyone of my brothers and sisters had their favorite act. My favorite act was the tightrope walkers. I was always fascinated by the fact that they could walk on the tightrope and not fall off. It took me years to figure out, that the key factor in tightrope walking, was the flexibility of the poles holding up the tightrope.

A relationship is much like tightrope walking. If a relationship is to work, both partners have to stand independently of each other, and, yet have total flexibility, just like the tightrope poles. It is this perfect balance and flexibility, between partners that maintains a relationship in spite of the problems that prance on the tightrope of life. If one partner is inflexible, the other partner is destined to be thrown to the ground or catapulted into space with the first crisis. If the partners are flexible like the tightrope poles, walking the tightrope of life isn't that difficult. It just takes practice and practice makes for a perfect relationship.

I love you, Mom

Dear Love,

There are two words among many in the English language that sound identical, but have diametrically opposite meanings. The words are "hole" and "whole". The word "hole" means empty and the word "whole" means filled.

When we are born we are born in "hole-ness". Our journey in life is toward "whole-ness." If life were idyllic, filling the "hole-ness" would be an easy process. However, very few people have idyllic families, schools, friends and life experiences. As a result, along the journey, as much as we try to fill in our "hole-ness," things happen that punch more holes in our developing "whole-ness."

It is a monumental task to struggle toward "whole-ness" with the constant erupting holes that invade our lives. However, the task is worthwhile. "Wholeness" comes when there is a sense that the absence or presence of people, circumstances and things in our lives, no longer completes who we are. We are complete when we can stand independently and alone, if necessary. With "whole-ness" comes peace.

I love you, Mom

Dear Love,

I have always loved the Christmas season. Shopping for Christmas was a job that began almost a year before the actual date. I would shop the end of the season bargains in January and February, to stock pile things at a very reasonable price, that I knew that I could not afford at full retail price the following Christmas time. I enjoyed all the thought and laughter that this brought to me, as I would tuck away little things and big things for the following year.

After Thanksgiving, I would take out the treasures that I had been hoarding all year and carefully wrap every single item to arrange under the Christmas tree as the day approached. I always enjoyed watching you open everything on Christmas morning and laughing at some of the Christmas things I had bought.

This year was so different for me. I have not been in any stores for months, for fear that I would buy anything. I cannot afford to send out Christmas cards, or even have a bowl of Christmas candy on the table. There are no presents of any kind. It has been a hard year financially.

I was feeling particularly down about this situation, as I was pouring over the normal household bills that I could not pay, and wondering what no presents at Christmas time would be like for you for the first time in your life. Would you be upset? or hurt? or angry at me? You must have been reading my mind, because you came bounding down the stairs, wrapped your arms around my neck, and said, "Mom, Christmas isn't about presents. It's about love — and we have enough for a lifetime." This was the most wonderful Christmas gift I could have ever received.

I love you, Mom